Contents

Introduction

This book could serve as an introduction to the topic of professional crime as it was in the first half of the twentieth century. An important part of this book is the following of gang activities through the newspapers, describing events as they were portrayed at the time. These were the sections I enjoyed writing the most and they are presented throughout the book in the relevant chapters.

We start in London, the largest city with the most crime stories, the most gangs, and the most wealthy targets for those gangs. We look at how gangs and individuals targeted horse racing, boxing and other sports. I really wanted to shine a light on the provincial English cities that also had their problems with gangs, as well as Glasgow, Belfast and Dublin. So many newspaper articles of the time compared our local gangs with those in America, and it was usually Chicago they chose, so there is a chapter on America including Al Capone and Bonnie and Clyde, because no book on gangs can fully set the context without them. We look at prison life, because it is interesting and was an important part of the life of a career criminal, and because so many gang accounts omit or gloss over it. We also look at the social context of the times, to help understand what drove people to crime and how gangs developed and sustained themselves. We look at the weapons the gang members chose, and why they almost always avoided using guns. The chapters on female criminals and gangs were also something I chose to include early on, because so few gang stories try to cover their activities which were in many cases even more cunning and audacious than the more numerous male gangsters.

You will find mention of some of the more famous career criminals such as the Sabinis, Billy Kimber, George Sage, the Cortesis, the Gilberts, the McDonalds and Alf Solomon. But I also signpost you to books that have covered their activities in great detail already.

I thoroughly enjoyed researching and writing this book, and uncovering some lesser-known gang stories. I hope you enjoy the journey too.

Chapter 1

London Gangs: An Introduction

It has been said that, in his day, Billy Kimber was the biggest and most successful organized crime boss in Britain. That is quite a claim. Billy's day lasted a couple of decades. He gradually came to prominence as a crime boss in the years after 1910, when the Great War threatened his ambitions. By 1914 he had made his name at the racetracks of England. Although he claimed to be a bookmaker, his services and related activities were mainly illegal. Of course, there was the occasional call for violence to maintain order. This will quickly become a tale of contradictions, of grey areas and divided loyalties. Welcome to gangland.

The Great War cleared away an old order, and fostered feelings of exhilaration for those who survived. It led to the Roaring Twenties, an idea powerful still today. But it did something else. It gave an entire generation of young men the skills to kill and use guns. It militarized a generation that came to find extreme violence normal. Not for everyone, of course, but for hundreds of angry young men in the largest cities of Britain and Ireland, it gave them what skills they needed to raise hell at home. Many tried, and many formed gangs to increase their power and influence. Some of those men became leaders within those gangs.

Although the richest punters and the fanciest clubs and bars were in the West End, many of the most ruthless and notorious gangs came from south of the river Thames. The Elephant Boys was more like a consortium than a single gang, and the McDonald family was a core of this scene throughout the twentieth century. One of the most famous McDonalds, Charles 'Wag' McDonald, left some diaries which have been incorporated in books published by his descendant, Brian McDonald. His book, *Elephant Boys*, is a lively account of his ancestors.

Any Londoner would guess that the Elephant Boys took their name from the area around Southwark, Walworth and Borough known as Elephant & Castle, the southern tip of the Bakerloo line. In the middle lies a huge road junction, not quite a roundabout, that draws comparison to Piccadilly Circus. The name itself most likely comes from the crest of the Worshipful Company of Cutlers which features a large elephant with a castle seated on its back. However, there has been a coaching inn or pub named Elephant & Castle in the area since the eighteenth century, which likely helped the name to stick.

There were thirteen McDonald siblings, of whom nine were boys, and many of them fought in the Boer War as well as the Great War. Their father, William, died young in 1896 and times were hard for the family. William Junior was twenty-five when his father died and he did try to lead by example as head of the family, enforcing discipline on his younger siblings. Charles, or Wag, is one of the most illustrious and best-remembered brothers, partly through his diaries. Brian McDonald's father was Charles's brother, Jim. Brian clearly remembers his uncle Wag, which adds even more colour to his writing. It was Billy Kimber himself who led the Elephant Boys at this time, and the McDonald brothers spent many hours in his company. It is understood that Billy would have been a father figure to these impressionable young men. Jim worked with Kimber at Kempton Park races, and Wag managed some illegal street pitches around the Elephant. Kimber's racecourse shenanigans led to him being forced out of the scene, which might have contributed to him enlisting for the Great War in 1916.

After Kimber left London, Wag emerged as the leader of the Elephant Boys through brute force and fighting. Kimber would return to London, but his chaotic empire was unmanageable, and he found Charles 'Darby' Sabini stepping in to take advantage. There were many brutal mass fights between followers of Kimber and Sabini as they struggled for advantage throughout the 1920s.

These feuds became so serious that Darby Sabini proposed a meeting at his home to negotiate a truce. The event was ill-advised and became a bad-tempered affair. In a fracas shortly after midnight, Billy Kimber was shot by Alf Solomon's pistol and needed hospital treatment.

This was Billy Kimber's most notorious episode and it resulted in him being shot during a fight in March 1921. The first the world knew about it, the newspapers were reporting that a bookmaker had been shot sometime after midnight on 27 March 1921. William Kimber, aged 37, had been found lying in the road outside 70 Collier Street near King's Cross railway station. The initial injuries appeared to be minor head wounds, but a bullet was soon found lodged in his side. Right from the off, Kimber was reluctant to discuss the events leading up to his shooting. Kimber's injuries were not life-threatening.

A day later, Tuesday 29 March, a man appeared at Clerkenwell Police Court before Judge Bros. The man was Alfred Solomon of Long Acre, also a bookmaker, aged twenty-seven. He was charged with causing Grievous Bodily Harm, not attempted murder, by shooting Billy Kimber with a revolver. A Detective Inspector Smith stated that the defendant gave himself up and made a written statement to the effect that Billy Kimber had been drunk and waved Kimber's own pistol at him, Alf Solomon. They struggled over the gun, causing it to discharge itself into Kimber's side. Solomon was remanded in prison for a week.

A week later, on 5 April, Solomon duly re-appeared at the same Clerkenwell Police Court. He was sticking to his story: the whole thing had been an unfortunate accident. The prosecution understandably claimed that the evidence for GBH against Solomon was thin. But more details were divulged by the *Nottingham Journal & Express* in their edition of 6 April. The fracas had ensued at the house of a Mrs Sabini. By this point, the press were describing the event as a 'drunken orgy'. Drinking continued until around 3.00am when a fight broke out. Glass was smashed. Kimber was still in hospital and unwilling to talk. Solomon was remanded for another week. The same day's *Yorkshire Post* implied that Billy Kimber was perfectly able to talk about the drunken orgy and his shooting, but chose not to. Again, the prosecution, in the person of a Mr Barker, stated that the incident was serious but the evidence was slender. Mr Barker, as quoted in the *Daily Herald* of 6 April, stated that it was Mrs Sabini's custom to offer alcohol to anyone present after licensing hours, a common theme among establishments frequented by Kimber and his boys. Mr Barker appeared frustrated by Kimber's reticence and suggested to the judge that Kimber be 'remanded' to appear before the court, a process apparently similar to the more famous *subpoena* process, rather than being remanded into prison, as had befallen Solomon, the accused.

By 18 April Billy Kimber had emerged from hospital and had finally been persuaded to give evidence. At this point, the story changed. Kimber's account of the night of 27 March agreed with the facts stated above until the point of the shooting. Kimber claimed that three men attacked him: one man hit him in the eye, a second man assaulted him, and a third man shot him. He did not know any of the men, he claimed. 'All I saw was a shadow,' said Kimber, as quoted by the *Westminster Gazette* of 19 April. Kimber did not have a gun himself and never saw anyone else with a gun. 'Only cowards carry revolvers,' said Kimber, who seemed reluctant to have the court blame Solomon for the crime. However, the judge decided to commit Solomon for trial for Grievous Bodily Harm.

When the appropriate people arrived at the Old Bailey for the trial itself, all except Alf Solomon were in for a disappointment. Mr Eustace Fulton appeared for the prosecution, offering only the flimsiest of evidence against Solomon. Solomon claimed the whole thing was an accident and Kimber offered nothing in response. Fulton described Kimber as the head of 'a Birmingham gang of terrors', and outlined the facts as described above. The judge, Mr Justice Darling, wasted no time in calling the trial off for lack of evidence. In essence, all the other witnesses were too drunk at the time to remember anything, Kimber forgot the whole episode, and Solomon claimed it was an accident. The judge directed the jury to return a not guilty verdict, and everyone went home.

As well as his association with the horse-racing gangs, Billy Kimber was also remembered by the infamous nightclub owner Kate Meyrick.

He worked for her for a time as an enforcer and strongman. Her most famous club was perhaps the *43* at 43 Gerrard Street, Soho. It became famous for all the wrong reasons, and Meyrick was often fined and even imprisoned for allowing drinking outside licensed hours. The 43 became so famous that its name is still used today for clubs around the country, in honour of the debauched original. However, the truth about Kate Meyrick's story, as so often in life, is less clear cut than this brief summary. Her story, told in her own words in *Secrets of the 43*, makes for a fascinating account of the nightclub scene during this time.

Soho in London, an area east of Regent Street and south of Oxford Street, running east as far as Tottenham Court Road, is a vibrant tourist trap. Luxury shops such as Liberty have stood there since 1875, together with Hamley's world-famous toy shop in Regent Street since 1881, perhaps marking the start of the modern idea of Soho as a place to unwind and shop after work and at the weekends. On the southern edge, Shaftesbury Avenue gives a clue to another side of Soho: this part of it is firmly inside the West End theatre district. Playhouses like the Lyric, the Windmill, and the Apollo are synonymous with live entertainment. The Windmill had been a cinema when it opened in 1909 but it became a live theatre in 1931, putting it bang in the middle of Soho's most notorious period. The Windmill offered nude cabaret and revue shows almost as soon as it converted to a live venue, and a distinctive seedy reputation for Soho began to build. Drink, gambling and girls went together throughout the early twentieth century and Soho became notorious throughout London and beyond.

Kate Meyrick was born into a wealthy Irish family in August 1875. She admits having been an imaginative, forceful personality from a young age and had dreams of becoming a doctor. Perhaps such a dream was unachievable at that time, or perhaps Kate was just not quite as committed as she thought. She learned how to handle the young men who flattered her with attention by trial and error, but settled on Dr Ferdinand Meyrick, an ambitious doctor. The medical world had ensnared Kate, but not quite in the way she had planned. Ferdinand specialized in psychiatry, and his growing practice soon took them to London.

It is important to dwell a little longer on Kate's story for several reasons. It is inspiring and thrilling even today, and even more so considering the attitudes to women in business at that time. But it also shows that the male-dominated world of the gangs is supported and complemented by women. We cross Kate's path because Billy Kimber provided physical security to Kate at various times, but Kate's story is every bit as gripping as his.

Kate and her husband separated in 1918, coinciding with the end of the Great War, which perhaps played a part in the decision. Kate's foray into the nightclub business came about mainly by chance. She was nursing one of her daughters through a grave case of 'flu in London when she had an opportunity to get involved in a venture that was more like a tearoom than a nightclub. Although Kate was from a wealthy family, there had been a problem with some inheritance money and so she was not herself wealthy, but nevertheless had the means for a small business investment in her own name. This experience would help her develop the skills which would provide her livelihood after Ferdinand abandoned her eight children. What this business experience showed Kate early on was that people, and men especially, will spend virtually unlimited amounts of money on entertaining themselves and their friends. In her own words: 'Men will pay anything to be amused.'

Kate set up in business with a club called Dalton's, next door to the Alhambra Theatre in Leicester Square. It stood where the Odeon cinema is today. Dalton's was a moderate success at first but soon ran into serious trouble. It was an underground venue and became popular with the wrong sort. Gangsters and even less scrupulous customers began to gather there and there was trouble with the police. But these were unusual times. Last orders was at the early time of ten o'clock, and the laws around serving alcohol were strict. As Kate describes it, the police were sympathetic to clubs because even they thought the laws were too strict. It seems to have been virtually impossible for a club to make a legitimate profit at a time when their main commodity, alcohol, had to be locked away at ten in the evening. So the police turned a blind eye to many things, but they could be mercurial in the way they chose to raid one property or another, and when, and on what pretext. It made the whole business seem very precarious to Kate Meyrick, but she found the lure of nighttime entertainment impossible to resist. It was a quick way to make enough money to support her large family. And Kate was, before anything else, a good mother.

An interesting phrase enters Kate's story at this point: the racecourse terrorist. The word terrorist today has very specific connotations to do with political violence of a grand kind, designed to catch the eye of the camera lens. Back then, the word had a much wider meaning. Very few gangsters carried guns, for reasons we will look at later on, and they did not have access to the advanced weapons used by terrorists today. So their terrorism was a more personal activity, and not necessarily with a political motive. From Kate's story, the word terrorist appears interchangeable with the word gangster, and this pattern is repeated in other sources from that time.

Kate soon found that she had no allies when it came to standing firm against the gangsters who chose her venues to refresh their thirst. They would arrive in groups, drink for hours and then leave without paying. Kate's staff were reluctant to involve the police. One night, she sent a man out to find a policeman to handle a difficult situation. He returned emptyhanded, and there is a suggestion that he had deliberately failed to find an officer. She sends him out once more, and he disappears into the night, never to return. The police did not want to get involved, and the staff did not want to be seen to be standing up to the gangsters. Staff members involved in any kind of controversy or publicity from the clubs would leave very quickly. There was a constant problem with recruiting and keeping staff in all roles, from the girls to bar staff and in particular the porters and bouncers.

The gangs were violent and anti-social, but they always had their code. It was rare for any of them to act violently towards women, and

Kate herself seemed largely immune to their threats, until one evening. Kate herself tried to refuse admission to a group of men. When one of them tried to elbow his way past her, she rushed him, and he attacked her, kicking her unconscious as she lay on the ground. Kate was lucky that night but was astonished when one of the other men in the group returned the next night to apologize. The gang's leader had given the perpetrator the hiding of his life for attacking Kate, and there was no more trouble from that group.

Dalton's went into decline and closed, and Kate tried a couple of other ventures in London. But soon her luck would change. The complications around her inheritance were resolved, and she found herself able to buy a much larger venue, at 43 Gerrard Street. Coincidentally, Kate had been 43 when she separated from her husband. The club quickly attracted an artistic and literary crowd, including Joseph Conrad in his last years, writer of *Heart of Darkness*. J.B. Priestley and his wife would visit occasionally. Even visiting American millionaires could be found at the 43. There was a darker side. Kate Meyrick states that 'London was just as bad as Chicago' in those days. She claims that police officers routinely dodged approaching gangs, offering no protection to the public. Some men who had been stabbed would be spirited away by friends to avoid the attentions of the press and police. Kate and other nightclub owners had to take protection into their own hands, not merely with the ever-present doormen but also a 'gigantic' porter who wielded an equally frightening hammer, whirling it around his head to deter even the more determined gang members. The system was not foolproof, and occasionally slip-ups presented danger. One night when Kate Meyrick was sitting alone in the office at the 43, a man appeared at the window with a revolver. 'What have you got, please?' he enquired politely, pointing his weapon. Kate Meyrick thought the man looked pleasant and failed to realize the gun was real. Smiling back at him, she pushed the muzzle towards the ceiling, and the gun discharged. The man ran immediately and the staff flooded in to check Kate was unharmed. The gunman had already held them up to gain access to the club, and

Kate's colleagues admired her bravery which she characteristically played down as ignorance of the danger in front of her.

Kate Meyrick rode her luck as a woman in a man's world and was at the helm of a wildly successful and popular nightspot by 1924. This was the year her luck ran dry, and a particularly dark and unpleasant period in her life is glanced over in her memoir. We understand that she is arrested, tried and sentenced to six months in prison, but the offence is not clearly explained. As best we can understand, she has violated the terms of her alcohol licence. At that time, such a misdemeanour would have been enough to incur a long stretch inside but the episode precipitated a decline in both Kate Meyrick's fortunes and her health.

She opens the chapter on her stay in Holloway Prison with a description of the appalling food. Breakfast was prison bread, which was either raw dough or as hard as granite, washed down with cold weak tea. The other meals were even worse. Those were the years of capital punishment, and a particularly gruesome execution that occurred a year before Kate Meyrick arrived at Holloway is related to her. The hanging of Edith Thompson was so traumatic that hardened prisoners claimed that the dread induced by Edith's shrieks would never leave their memories. Her grave was to be found beneath a clump of bushes in the prisoner's exercise area.

The doors of Holloway soon opened to let Kate Meyrick out. A well-meaning financier customer offered her a loan of up to fifty thousand pounds which in the 1920s was an even more generous amount than it would be today, certainly over a million pounds. The only catch was that she had to invest it in what he determined to be 'legitimate' businesses, by which he meant anything but nightclubs.

Within a month of leaving Holloway, Kate Meyrick had brushed aside this offer and opened a new club in Golden Square, Soho. Known simply as *The Little Club*, it was popular from the start. The 43 was still in business. Kate was expanding her empire. The actress Tallulah Bankhead and Frederick Lonsdale, a successful playwright, were customers. Michael Arlen, then a famous novelist whose books including *The Green Hat* had been made into films, also visited. Despite his English-sounding name, Arlen was really a Bulgarian by the name of Dikran Kouyoumdjian. Nobody and nothing was what it seemed in Soho.

Finally, the harassment of the police became too much and Kate Meyrick left London for a time. In June 1925 she moved to Paris to open clubs there, leaving the London clubs in the hands of others. She returned that October to find that they had continued as successful businesses without her. This gave her the confidence to open the *Manhattan* club in Denman Street. Meyrick was riding high on business success. Rudolph Valentino made the 43 his first port of call on any visit to London. May 1927 brought the opening in Regent Street of the *Silver Slipper* club with its iconic and eye-catching illuminated glass dancefloor. Sadly, the glass was not up to the job and it cracked one night as Tallulah Bankhead and Prince Nicholas of Romania danced the night away.

Kate Meyrick would return to Holloway Prison. Her first six-month sentence was followed by another of the same length, and her third stint was particularly tough: a fifteen-month sentence. She left in January 1930, only to return that summer for a fourth stint. She returned again in May 1931 for her fifth and final stint. Remember that in each case the misdemeanour was the infringement of her alcohol licence only. In total Kate Meyrick spent three years and three months in prison for serving drinks after hours.

Kate Meyrick's book is a delight that entertains and informs all these years after it was written in 1933, just before another war became inevitable. She died before it was published, and it is a fitting tribute to a difficult but exciting life. It shines light far beyond her nightclubs. It lets us see into a single life in great detail, with all of the attitudes and fears of the times Kate lived through. The most striking sentence for us is that one about London being as bad as Chicago. It is a common comparison that we see across many sources from the time, but as far as we can see from this distance, it is false. This belief shows us that Chicago had a huge myth around it even a century ago, but it also shows us that people across the British Isles were worried about levels of violence in our major cities. No doubt not every event in this book unfolded in precisely the way Kate Meyrick remembers: there is some embellishment involved, but the book is no less wonderful or useful for that. Kate Meyrick was a successful woman in a man's world, and the story of our gangs needs more of the female perspective.

Chapter 2

London Gangs in the Newspapers

People talk of the media today to include not only newspapers, radio and television, but also the streaming services, internet news and magazines, apps and no doubt other novelties yet to be invented. If anyone had used the word 'media' between the wars, they would most likely have been thinking only of newspapers and, possibly, books. Radio was just coming into use as a way to communicate to large audiences. It was 1922 before the BBC got up and running, under a licence from the post office, which underlines the idea that radio was seen as a similar communication medium to the written letter and reflects its origins in the telegraph which had been used for sending telegrams: the historical counterpart most similar to today's emails and text messages.

The newspapers of the time did not strive for ease of understanding. Nothing was printed in colour. There were few photographs and the printers were intent on saving paper. Columns were crammed together, often unbroken in their relentless gasping urgency to convey their stories. Even the front page was crammed with tiny text. They were daunting prospects for most people to persevere with, but they were the only reliable source of distant happenings.

Although the common idea of an old newspaper is overwhelmingly the unwieldy broadsheet, the *Daily Mirror* became the first daily tabloid as early as 1903. It incorporated titillating crime stories from the first moment. Apart from its lack of colour, its design was much easier to read and the stories were told in shorter sentences. The blueprint for today's newspapers has not changed much, testimony to the basic soundness of the design: a bold title with eye-catching graphical blocks either side, and gigantic front-page headlines designed to persuade you to buy, even if you glanced from across the busy train station. There were far more photographs than traditional newspapers. They were designed as an entertainment medium as much as a news one. So we have the context in which the authorities could communicate with a mass audience.

It is therefore newspapers that make the most reliable and contemporary source of information about the gang leaders of the early twentieth century. Notwithstanding their eye for scandal and sensation, they were usually right on the basic facts. For a combination of other reasons, the working classes could only expect their lives to appear in print if their behaviour grabbed the attention of journalists. No time to write long, flowing love letters, no time for straining each night at a diary, they were intent on survival in terms of making enough money and avoiding or surviving violence. The working classes had to rely on journalists to write their stories for them, but at least we have the newspapers.

The British Newspaper Archive is a brilliant resource for older newspapers around the country, and a search for 'London gangs' shows at a quick glance how prevalent that phrase is at various times in our country's history. By far the greatest number of references occurred between 1850 and 1899, with over 588,000 logged. Usually, one reference is one article. There were roughly half as many entries for the period of this book, from 1900 to 1949, and just under 200,000 for the second half of the twentieth century, although it must be remembered that the archive is still being completed for the years since 1950. Nevertheless, this gives a very good broad indication about how much gang activity was affecting the public conscience at various times.

Focusing on the first half of the 1900s, we find a reduction in the number of articles during the second world war years. From 1940 to 1949 there were only 34,000 articles compared to 63,000 in the decade to 1939 and 97,000 in the first decade of the century to 1910.

Another reason for mentioning this, apart from seeing roughly how interested the newspapers were in gangs at various times, and an indication of peaks and troughs in gang activity too, is that it demonstrates how any selection of articles about London gangs during these decades is going to be subjective. In all of my rewarding weeks gleaning snippets from the archives, I had an eye out for 'typical' or indicative stories of the general feeling of the time, but also for unusual stories, whether they be particularly exciting, tragic, humorous or whatever grabbed my attention on that day in history.

The first reference that caught my eye in relation to crime and gangs in the new century was, surprisingly, in *The Queen*, which described itself as the Lady's Newspaper. In November of 1900, *The Queen* published a wide column and a half on the state of law enforcement. It makes an important point which is in abrupt contrast to modern policing: 'as at present administered, the law treats crimes against property much more severely than crimes against the person.' The exact opposite is the case today, and although many burglary victims are reportedly frustrated at not being able to interest the police, even those victims would tend to agree that personal injury should be treated more seriously. As the article makes clear, 'The property of which a man is robbed may be replaced by him with a few hours or days of extra labour.'

This principle is important in understanding many of the cases in London and throughout Britain at this time. It was puzzling to me that the theft of a few cigarettes could lead to several months in prison with hard labour, a penalty that seemed extreme for such a minor crime. The sentences mirrored society, and it is clear that honesty and property were protected more thoroughly than mere flesh and blood. It is also clear that flesh belonging to the upper and middle classes was protected better than that belonging to the working classes. A street fight involving working men might involve a small fine and a few days in prison, for example, even if knives were used.

The article deploys the logic that too severe a punishment might lead to brutalizing the offender and making it impossible to rehabilitate him. It goes on to cherry-pick certain cases which highlight the points being made, including the lenient sentence of caning for teenagers found placing stones on a railway with the intent to derail the train, with the potential for huge loss of life. The law tends to punish actual consequences rather than intended ones, and the driver of the train managed to stop it safely before hitting the obstruction. The more detailed case described in the article refers to the brutal sexual assault of a girl under the age of sixteen, a domestic servant. The gang of eight youths involved in the crime were given sentences ranging from six months to a year with hard labour but, the article notes, 'A few years since such an act as was committed by these scoundrels could have been punished by death.' The article also shows an awareness that not all victims and not all offenders are created equal. Would the punishment have been more severe if the domestic servant had been a lady of the manor? 'Had the case occurred in the United States, and the criminals been negroes, there is not the slightest doubt that the general feeling of the community would have led, at least in many districts, to the breaking open the jail and the execution by lynch law of the whole of the prisoners.'

Finally, the article comes to the topic of gangs, which at the time were frequently referred to as ruffians or hooligans, terms which have diluted meaning today and tend to imply minor offences. But in 1900 a ruffian could easily be a professional gangster who had slashed open the face or neck of an opponent with a razor. Meanwhile the word hooligan was also used to describe hordes of people involved in riots, whether as part of a political protest or strike action. But then, even the term riot was misleading as it could also be applied to a gang brawl or street fight.

This article, a one-sided editorial, shows some of the thoughts in the minds of their readers as the new century began. We know that prison was not the idyllic recuperation hotel implied in this article, and that the food was diabolical. We know that later on, gang members were in fact treated more severely by the courts than 'normal' or lone criminals, but it feels like public opinion is swelling against criminals at this time, judging from editorials like this one and the sheer number of articles mentioning gangs in the early 1900s. It is important to note that attitudes to the punishment and to the criminals, and the adjustment of punishing crimes against the person more severely than theft or burglary, was all about to change significantly.

In July 1908 *The Yorkshire Telegraph and Star* gleefully related some trouble in London involving 'Expert gangs of American and Continental thieves ... .' The improbably-named American, General Drain, who was looking after the American Olympic shooting team, suffered the theft of a jewel case from his room in the Hotel Victoria on Northumberland Avenue. The jewel case contained numerous items, including diamonds and an Olympic medal. There followed a list of numerous jewel robberies from high-end visitors in expensive hotels with no suspects named. A series of similar articles appeared throughout 1907 and 1908 as the size and frequency of the gang's raids showed confidence and genuine skill that repeatedly thwarted the police.

On 28 May 1911, *Lloyd's Weekly News* reported on two stories that show the different types of gangs at work on London's streets: one professionally organized by well-planned and calculating groups, operating with great skill and the other, more spontaneous and less planned, often requiring some actual or implied violence. The paper worried that the meticulously planned burglaries from high-end West End jewellers were on the rise.

On Heddon Street, a cul-de-sac off Regent Street, a gang entered the premises of a wholesale manufacturer of silverware late on Thursday afternoon when the premises were empty. They were then able to work as many hours into the night as they needed and stole £200 of high quality goods. The staff were not aware of the burglary until they arrived for work on the Friday morning and raised the alarm. Contrast this to a foiled burglary attempt by a lone smash-and-grab operator. As the night watchman was patrolling a silversmith's on the corner of Regent Street and Jermyn Street, he heard 'three heavy blows and the crash of glass at one of the shop windows just above his head. Looking up through a grating, he saw a short, stoutly built man in the act of throwing a brick at the window for a fourth time'. The burglar ran off when the watchman raised the alarm.

On the same day, the *Lloyd's Weekly News* reported a con trick perpetrated against a wealthy tourist, a tea planter from India. The man was approached by a friendly Australian and they spent some hours sightseeing. The Australian promised a trip by motor car the next day. 'He called, as arranged, at the [victim's] hotel, but without the car.' He then suggested they do more sightseeing on foot, and the Indian tourist brought with him a valuable camera. It soon emerged that the Australian was working with another man who pretended to be a complete stranger. He dropped a small velvet case in the street in front of them, and the victim immediately picked it up to return it. There followed a sob story in which the owner of the case explained he had to dispense £20,000 in charity as part of an undertaking in the will of his late father. For reasons not made clear in the article, this necessitated some 'proof of confidence' and the Australian man, in league with this new arrival, handed over what appeared to be bank notes. The victim went to his own bank for £200 which he then handed over also. Carrying the £200 and the valuable camera, the Australian and his accomplice departed to 'fetch from his bank the funds for distribution'. They never returned, and the victim slowly came to realize that he had been swindled. The episode is notable for the care and time taken to establish the trust of the victim, the intricacy of their ploy, and the gullibility of quite wealthy tourists to the West End.

In September 1911, there was an altercation between rival gangs who had regularly been causing trouble around Shoreditch and Bethnal Green, at the corner of Hackney Road and Shoreditch High Street. The fracas saw knives wielded and a gun was witnessed although not fired. However, it was the sequel that attracted headlines. As two gang members were being held in a police station for charges in relation to the fight, eight men from the rival gang, some of them holding loaded guns, rushed into the police station and attacked the two defendants. The report in the *Belfast Evening Telegraph* of 23 September 1911 is confusing about whether the ambush happened inside the police station or on the steps outside, as the two accused were being led away by police.

But the substance of the incident is clear: gang members were prepared to wield pistols and attack prisoners even when they were being guarded by police. The Old Street magistrate was disgusted: 'To think that in the middle of London, in the heart of a civilized country, people should wait on the steps of a police court with loaded revolvers in their pockets, for other men to come out, in order to make an organized attack on them, is almost incredible.' Certainly cold heads would consider the ambush idiotic, but it shows both that guns were in fairly widespread use in London at the time, and feelings were running high enough between the two gangs that eight of them would risk immediate arrest to carry out reprisals.

In July 1914, an article appeared in the *Nottingham Daily Express* which showed how far afield the London racing gangs might operate. Three members of a gang travelled to the Long Eaton Recreation Ground near Nottingham where races were being held. The three men all pleaded guilty to 'loitering with intent to commit a felony' after a witness, Arthur Edward Singleton, had grabbed one of the men's hands as it tried to lift his wallet from his trouser pocket. A police constable had seen this event and appeared as a witness. The sentences, three months' hard labour for each man, seem harsh, especially with guilty pleas, but this was due to a long list of earlier crimes. One of the men had as many as thirteen prior convictions.

In September 1922 news of the notorious Sabini gang reached the *Lincolnshire Chronicle*. They also mentioned Thomas Gilbert, a name often linked to Birmingham's Peaky Blinders. The editorial article makes some vague claims about blackmail and robbery but does not mention specific incidents. Their claim that the 'really dangerous gangs number four' yet they are 'from 300 to 500 strong' seems contradictory, or at least misleading, as it would have been impossible to closely organize such large gangs. Other sources suggest the gangs were more like loose affiliations and occasional collaborations, the gang members not being in a fixed organization that lasted for long periods. The article continues, 'Their great game is blackmail. Members of the gang make the acquaintance of people in high places, gradually make confidants of them, learn their secrets, and then turn around and demand a big price for secrecy.' The blackmailers also lured in 'pretty girls' who they would encourage to befriend 'young men about town' and lure them away to quiet places to be robbed or conned at cards.

The calculating focus on the upper classes is noteworthy and logical. The richer the victim, the more money could be made, of course, but there is a more subtle attraction. Someone of standing, or a member of the aristocracy, would go to lengths to avoid their name appearing in the papers. Even less attractive to be named as someone who could easily be tricked at cards or lured in by a complete stranger. Such people were less likely to report the crimes and were more able to withstand the losses.

As if to underline this point, the *Evening Telegraph* brought news in April 1923 that a country house in Woking had become the latest target of London burglary gangs. 'Following several recent cases in which the methods employed were characteristic of two London "gangs," consultations have taken place between police officers from Woking and members of the Yard's "flying squad," who are provided with a fast motor car.' Embarrassingly, the house they targeted, The Rydens in Mount Hermon Road, was only a few hundred yards from a police station. The thieves used bell ropes and eiderdowns stolen from the house in which to tie up and carry away clothing and jewellery. In response, the police were blocking roads into London and checking cars they stopped.

Such burglaries were supposed to be safe and non-violent ways to make large amounts of money but, occasionally, disasters happened. In May 1925 the *Dundee Evening Telegraph and Post* brought news of a police car chase. This was front-page news and would have been a comparatively rare event at the time. A gang of five London burglars, who had been operating around Stroud in Gloucestershire, drove past a police station and were seen by a Superintendent Lane. The police gave chase in their own car and caught up with the burglars at a garage. The two cars almost crashed on a hill before the burglars 'mounted a path, turned completely over, and two men were found dead underneath, while three others escaped in the darkness over a field, and are still at large.'

News of the feud between the racing gangs spread as far as the *Londonderry Sentinel* on the last day of August 1922. This time it was Fred Gilbert, brother of Thomas, and George Sage in the news but this time they were the target of pistol shots. The prosecution described how three full taxi-cabs containing a dozen gang members left Hurst Park races bound for Mornington Crescent. One of the shooters was named as Joseph Sabini, indicating that this attack was part of an spat between the Sabinis and the Gilberts. Various pistols and revolvers were in use, but one weapon in particular caught the attention of the prosecution: 'I have never seen a more dangerous weapon. It is half a six-chambered revolver and half a stiletto, and can be housed in an innocent-looking walking stick. It still bears on its point marks of blood it got on that night.' The gangs did sometimes use guns, but this is an extraordinary attempt at concealment.

In June 1925, Prince Henry opened a lads' club in Norwich, according to a small story in Bristol's *Western Daily Express*. This was a decade before his brother Edward would abdicate the British throne. The boys' club movement had attracted royal attention, even in the provinces, and this club had the express intention of improving the behaviour of local youths and helping them see the police in a more human light. Prince Henry was met by the Earl of Leicester and the organizer of the new club, Chief Constable Dain. In his speech, the Prince said that the club 'had taught boys to look upon the police as their friends. The police and boys are on such friendly terms that I should not be surprised to hear that in the near future the city police have ceased to exist owing to the good behaviour of the rising generation of citizens.'

March 1931 and the *Sheffield Independent* brought news of a successful burglary at the London home of Lord Stanley of Alderley in Grosvenor Square. Thieves had gained access through an upper-storey window by making use of footholds found in stone carvings on a wall. When a servant in the basement heard a noise and came to check, the thieves made their escape using 'an improvised rope of webbing such as is used by upholsterers' which they tied to a balustrade on the second floor. The servant could find no trace of them, or of thousands of pounds worth of property.

On the very same page of the *Sheffield Independent* of 26 March 1931 is the headline 'Baby-Faced Girl Bandit', which leads an article about a girl with 'dark bobbed hair, a small innocent-looking face and an active and intelligent brain'. The unnamed girl had the last laugh over this patronizing description because she had already netted thousands of pounds from various other country house burglaries. In other smaller crimes such as bag snatching she has assisted as a chauffeur of a stolen car. 'She is an expert motor driver,' is the admiring aside. A girl fitting this description had also been part of a bandit gang that had been broken up by police, but without apprehending the girl with a bob. In those times she was known as 'Queen of the Soho Gang' but was never named.

In October 1937, breaking into country houses was still a newsworthy item. Three men were sent to prison for breaking into a house in Gerrards Cross, Buckinghamshire. The Chairman of the Buckinghamshire Quarter Sessions intended to make an example of the group: 'He emphasized the seriousness of young London gangs thinking they could get "quick money" in Bucks by stripping empty houses.' Although in this case the property in question was only one pair of gold cufflinks. Leslie George Goodwin, a twenty-five year-old chef, admitted to being the ringleader and was said to have 'a number' of previous convictions. He got the longest sentence of one year with hard labour.

In March 1938 several skirmishes between two gangs began on a Saturday night when members of an unnamed Soho gang drove two large cars around Finsbury to reconnoitre the area. They were preparing an attack on another gang and returned the following afternoon when a small fight broke out but, at pub closing time on the Sunday night, chaos erupted. The cars disgorged eight occupants who, as reported by the *Daily Herald*, went into a hotel bar. Another man, his allegiances unclear, telephoned for reinforcements and, before long, twenty men were involved in a full-scale affray. The episode is notable for the amount of trouble the Soho gang went to in preparing their ambush, and also for the use of at least one blade in the fight, described as a 'Scimitar'. Other weapons included 'swords, hatchets, bars of iron and rods of glass'. No firearms were present.

One hallmark of the 1930s' crimes in and around London was the increasing use of private motor vehicles to travel to more remote locations and as getaway vehicles. Not only were these more discreet than public transport, allowing the occupants to evade eyewitnesses, but they were easy to steal and could be abandoned afterwards.

One of the most striking gangland episodes in 1940s London was the murder by stabbing of one Harry 'Scarface Hubby' Distleman in a Wardour Street bridge and billiards club. All of the involved were gangsters involved in running clubs or protection rackets and there was a dispute early in the evening which resulted in associates Distleman and Edward Fletcher being thrown out, only to return later on. The case became famous because, although it eventually resulted in the execution of the perpetrator, Antonio 'Babe' Mancini, his appeal was heard three times in total, including in the House of Lords. His case was the first murder appeal to be heard so many times, and he became the first London gangster to be executed 'for at least 20 years'.

The episode appears to have been a general affray that got out of hand. Mancini claimed self-defence and that he had no intention of stabbing Distleman. He said he had found a knife on the floor but later admitted to having brought it into the club himself, disguised with a piece of cloth. A man called Edward Fletcher was also seriously injured, and the three men had known each other for fifteen years or more. The most detailed account I could find was in the *Shields Daily News* in Northumberland for 16 May 1941. Mancini changed his statements more than once and admitted fighting with Fletcher. He said that 'Fletcher saw me and made for me with a raised chair.' He went on to claim that he was trying to mediate in a fight between Fletcher and others but perhaps a more reliable witness was Patrick Crowley, a doorman at the club. He said that 'Mancini and Fletcher were involved in a struggle when Distleman intervened. Mancini pushed Distleman away and continued his fight with Fletcher.' If this is true, then Distleman was unlucky indeed and it becomes clear why various courts agonized over the conviction of Mancini for murder. Whether or not he brought his own knife with him that night, all accounts agree that it was more of a brawl than a premeditated attack, and that Distleman was more or less a bystander. However, if the House of Lords were to overturn the conviction, they would have to let Mancini walk free. There was no option for them to change the sentence to prison or hard labour, for example, or to reduce the charge to manslaughter. It was either execution or exoneration. Antonio Mancini was hanged in Pentonville Prison on 31 October 1941 by notorious hangman Albert Pierrepoint.

After the war, in February 1946, Scotland Yard arrested fifty members of burglary gangs in one day after an intelligence-gathering crackdown the previous December during which they had cordoned off parts of the West End and stopped 'thousands' of passersby. The police retrieved thousands of pounds' worth of furs and jewellery, plus 'eight revolvers and a big quantity of ammunition' and tools for housebreaking, according to the *Belfast News-Letter*.

April 1947 brought a less typical story about London vice gangs 'importing wives' from overseas to be used in sex work. One of the victims explained how the system worked to a journalist from the *London News Chronicle*: 'As much as £100 has been paid to Englishmen in Italy and France to marry women so that the women can obtain British nationality and come to England to work for the gang bosses. After they arrive a divorce is arranged and is paid for by the gangsters so that the "husband" is put to no expense and makes a fair profit out of a woman he sees only once.' The gang consisted of five Maltese men most of whom received sentences of four years' penal servitude. This allowed the judge to make the dubious criticism, not limited to the five defendants before him, that 'there are in this country, and supported by this country, a great number of people who were born elsewhere and who do nothing for the support of this country ... . I think it is desirable that attention should be drawn to the fact, in view of the difficulties of this country at the present time.'

Also in 1947 the *Hull Daily Mail* highlighted a problem similar to that seen after the Great war in 1918. 'A number of deserters, some foreigners, who are known to be members of London gangs, are believed to be armed, and even sell from a store to other criminals.' For a minority of those leaving the armed forces, firearms were useful in carrying out crimes and also had a street value.

The *Hull Daily Mail* was again happy to report on London's troubles in the summer of 1949. The previous year's annual report by the Commissioner of Police in London had just been published. In 1948, compared to 1947, 'there is an increase of nearly 28 per cent more children (8–13), 21 per cent more persons between 14 and 16, and four per cent more persons between 17 to 20, arrested for indictable crimes. In all there was an increase of 1,669 or 16.7 per cent in arrests of persons under 21.' The increase in the ten years after 1938 was only fifty per cent altogether, with all the temptations brought by its chaos including absent parents, which meant there were around 10,000 arrests of such young people in 1948, and that the situation was worsening even years after the war had ended. The Commissioner of Police, Sir Harold Scott, blamed the courts for handing down lenient probation instead of prison. Ninety per cent of young people arrested were male. And this worsening in youth crime was in contrast to a generally falling crime rate.

Chapter 3

The Horse Racing Gangs

D ick Kirby is a former Metropolitan Police officer who has written extensively about London's underworld. He brings up the name Billy Kimber in the introduction to *The Racetrack Gangs*. Although horse racing has always been synonymous with gambling, it has never in recent times been associated with incessant crime. If you think of a sport known for its violence away from the field of play, you are most likely to think of football and its attendant hooligans. So how did the horse racing community find itself menaced by gangs up and down the country?

It all started at a long-gone type of venue in London known as the pleasure gardens. You cannot relive the full pleasure garden experience today, but some of them still exist as parks. Vauxhall Pleasure Garden, in the shadow of the current MI6 spy headquarters, has been a place to stroll since before 1660 but it became a fully-fledged venue for pleasure in 1785, and it was in those years that it really earned its reputation. It was known as a public entertainment venue right up until the mid-nineteenth century. Then known as New Spring Gardens, it could handle vast crowds. In 1749, for example, 12,000 people flocked to watch a rehearsal of Handel's *Music for the Royal Fireworks* but this crowd was dwarfed in 1786 by a fancy-dress jubilee that attracted 61,000 London revellers. The main paths were lined with lamps, a novelty back then, and there were rococo pavilions, arches and statues. This mix of green space with grand architecture, all illuminated and with a background of live music, was intoxicating. As you might expect for the times, such large crowds were a magnet for small-time crooks. The pleasure garden was a place to be seen, to flash your status, and to share gossip, but it was open to all, with the entry price of one shilling being affordable by all layers of Britain's strict class-based society. It was also, enticingly, one of the few places where men and women could mix freely and a little furtively, if they needed to. Not all the paths were lit, and those darker paths were hotbeds of scandal and crime.

These gardens were not invented in London; they were European imports. However, they were immensely popular. At the height of the trend, there were over sixty in the capital. There were others in the USA, and even in Russia and Australia. It was only towards the end of the 1800s, as Billy Kimber was finding his way in Birmingham, that the public found the pleasure gardens becoming stale. The stylish classes drifted away first, but the lure of the music hall and seaside coincided with the arrival of the railways. To make matters even worse, land values rose as London expanded and the site of the gardens became too valuable to host evening parties. One of the beneficiaries of the trend for entertainment out of town, turbocharged by the railways, were the racecourses, and the pickpockets and con artists of the pleasure gardens gradually found a new home there.

An important reason for gangsters targeting the racecourses is that betting was only allowed at the tracks. Off-course betting shops were not allowed. So anyone wanting to profit from predicting the outcome of a race either had to physically travel to the track or somehow send bets to a bookmaker stationed at the track, typically by telephone. This deterred the casual punters. There were illegal street bookmakers but they were not strictly policed, and many managed to carry on a reasonable trade, but this put gambling away from the course outside the law, perhaps having the unexpected side effect of helping the gangs to flourish. A big race meeting like the Epsom Derby could see half a million spectators arriving in all manner of modern transport from trains to buses, cars and even on the more traditional horseback.

The more serious criminal activity was directed at those with the most cash to hand: the bookmakers. Gangs would demand protection money; they would threaten and intimidate bookmakers and steal their pitches.

Using all manner of crooked wheezes, the gangs could clear thousands of pounds at a big race meeting. It was good business but it was violent. Bookmakers had to be beaten up every so often so that they took the threats seriously. The catalyst for violence was that such profits attracted more gangs than there were bookmakers: the gangs sometimes fought amongst themselves over who was protecting which bookmakers.

The gangs thought nothing of resisting arrest with whatever weapons they had to hand. The police were seen as just another adversary, another form of gang to be resisted. The police had a special power in that they were backed by the courts and often sent gang members to prison for short stretches. The unluckier ones would be sent away for several years, so it is not surprising that gangs caught in a battle might temporarily unite against the police and co-operate to ensure that witnesses would be too frightened to show up at court.

Although guns are not such a feature of the British mob scene, as compared to America, they do pop up occasionally. The gang members all routinely carried knives, but guns were rare. Possession of a firearm, even an unused one, would add to your prison sentence.

Due to simple supply and demand, the gangs had to compete for the attentions of a bookmaker, and the bookmakers in turn would play the gangs off against each other. You might expect repeat offenders and gang members to be barred entry to the courses, and they were. But some races were held on common ground, a loophole that allowed even violent criminals access to the spectators and bookmakers. This situation proved particularly difficult to counteract using the technology of the time. In 1934 a simple form of helicopter, the autogyro, was used to police race meetings. But the drop in popularity of horse racing set in during the 1920s. The Great Depression was blamed for much of the damage, but the pernicious influence of the gangs was so widespread that they were also credited with harming the industry, frightening off legitimate punters.

Gangs of the turf, those who targeted punters and people working within horse racing, get prominent mention in stories about gangs of the 1920s and with good reason. Every era has its defining crime, the one which perfectly balances risk and reward, the crime that can yield the most money for the least effort and, in the 1920s in Britain and Ireland, it was at the races. Perhaps it was the equivalent of today's drug trade, or of moonshine alcohol in America during the prohibition era.

What horse racing had more than any other sport was gambling, and gambling brought cash, and in the early years of the twentieth century, horse racing was enormously popular. In the 1920s, crowds of 250,000 or more for the Epsom Derby were routine, and some claims suggest tens of thousands more than that, although all numbers were estimates. In 2019, a *Racing Post* article lamented how the crowds on Epsom Hill had dwindled in the prior decade. Although the hill area is free to attend and therefore crowd size can only be estimated, the ticketed areas sold only 36,000 that year. More strikingly, when compared with activities in the 1920s, there were only six arrests for minor offences.

Excitement drew the small-time gamblers of the expanding middle classes, and their cash drew the con artists and gangs from every major British city. The activities of the large, organized gangs of London and Birmingham have been well-documented by experts such as Dick Kirby and Carl Chinn, but there are hidden stories that are just as interesting. This chapter focuses on the heyday of the racing gangs in the 1920s.

The Sporting Times of July 1920 complained about 'racing ruffianism' and it is worth noting how important labels can be in public reaction to an event. To today's ear, a ruffian is not a terrifying prospect; it calls to mind a child misbehaving in some minor way. But in the 1920s the professional gang members were labelled ruffians and terrorists, and the two terms were used interchangeably.

The Sporting Times' piece is an editorial and is suggesting that other sporting papers were trying to suppress the problem of gang activity within horse racing, leaving it to the general papers to cover, and denying its existence themselves at every opportunity. It is important to realize that this discussion was going on, and to acknowledge that certain newspaper titles deemed to be closely involved in racing might be trying to play down the problem. The paper suggests that only corporal punishment would deter the gangs, and laments that the 'cat o'nine tails' was no longer in use. Dark reference is made to some major disturbance at Salisbury, and also Harnham Hill and Danebury, and notes that all these skirmishes happened at courses in the west country.

All the trouble occurred outside the ticketed enclosures, in the large crowds that could turn up without paying for a ticket. At this point the article takes a dark turn. They note 'trouble between Jew and gentile divisions' and claim that it 'is well known that the majority of the men who have been giving trouble of late are not British-born' under the heading 'Alien Outlaws'. Yes, these were different times in terms of the phrasing used but these were false claims too. The vast majority of those involved in gang violence were British-born. The paper was right in identifying the problem but then exploited public fears by blaming the wrong communities.

The paper suggested that the Jockey Club should create its own private security force to ensure public safety at their events, and they were right in anticipating that such a solution would one day come. At the time the Jockey Club simply shirked responsibility for any activities outside their official ticketed enclosures. The paper runs on for several columns, including the hypocrisy of the English punters who knowingly used unlicensed bookmakers both at the track and away from it, during a time when betting away from racecourses was illegal but not punished consistently by the authorities.

The Sunday Pictorial of 3 April 1921 brings shocking news of a shooting incident between 'Two Gangs of Terror Men' at Alexandra Park on Saturday 2nd. The disturbance was blamed on two gangs known vaguely as the 'Birmingham and Italian Gangs', and the latter usually referred to men associated with the Sabinis, although there were lesser-known Italian gangs, including the Cortesis.

The trouble continued into June when a man was arrested at Epsom racecourse with a loaded, unlicensed revolver. It seemed to police that he was walking along a line of bookmakers looking for a specific individual.

The article in the *Northern Daily Mail* specifically makes a connection to 'the shooting affair at Alexandra Park some weeks ago'. The man had no fewer than eighteen previous convictions and went to prison for three months, showing just how seriously firearms offences were taken, and explaining why so few people carried them.

On the way home from the same race meeting, two gangs were involved in a fight that drew a large number of witnesses because of its size. Twenty-eight men were charged in the end in a fight involving 'Hammers, Hatchets, Bottles and Bricks' and quite possibly firearms too. Photos accompanied the story. The gang had travelled in a charabanc motor-bus which was later apprehended near Ewell. The fight seems to have been between rival gangs from Leeds and Birmingham and led to six men going to hospital with head wounds. Eyewitness reports do not make it totally clear what happened, but the Leeds car and the Birmingham charabanc seem to have been deliberately driven into each other before fighting broke out. It shows that racecourse gang violence would spill out beyond the racecourse and put members of the public in harm's way. During this period, the 'racecourse wars' were at their height and it is clear that similar events over a short period of time forced the authorities to act.

The *Illustrated Police News* of 25 August brought news of a gang incident at Bath races. Violence broke out at the racecourse but also in other locations around Bath. The usual weapons including hammers and life-preservers were used. Five men were described as being 'seriously injured', of whom the name Alfred Solomon appeared first and most eye-catchingly. Solomon was said to suffer 'severe scalp wounds'. Four of the five were from London. The paper makes an unsubstantiated claim that an incredible 500 Birmingham gang members lay in wait at the railway station in Bath. It is unlikely that so many men would injure only five of the London gang and they would have been conspicuous due to the size of the group around that area. Three motor coaches were used to transport the Birmingham gang members around Bath while they used binoculars to spot their victims. Another article on the same page demonstrates that some firearms were present during the fracas, although none were fired. Alfred's brother, Henry Solomon, was sentenced to one month in prison for having an unlicensed revolver with intent to endanger life. He was claimed to be part of a 150-strong group which forced entry into the enclosure at Bath races that day. A witness in the case, George Wiley, had said he was intimidated at Waterloo station to discourage him from travelling to Bath to testify against Solomon in the case. The courts would hand out bigger sentences when gangs were caught tampering with witnesses.

28 August 1921 was an important day: the *Sunday Illustrated* was in a position to 'announce exclusively that a truce between the London and Birmingham gangs of racecourse pests has been effected.' This was not quite the unconditional ceasefire that the paper implied. Although each gang agreed that certain key members would not visit racecourses from that moment forwards, other papers reported simply that the gangs had agreed not to continue their vendettas on the racecourses themselves. It was clear that they were happy to continue their violence behind closed doors, or indeed anywhere else at all. This announcement came just three days after reports of the incidents at Bath racecourse described above.

The truce did not last. In *The Times* of 7 July 1921 a significant disturbance began in Salisbury after police arrested gang members at the railway station. 'A gang of around 50 men attempted to release the arrested men, who were placed in a motor omnibus … . Then the gang tried to stop a car containing police, and one man, who jumped in front of it, was knocked down. A fight ensued, and a constable in plain clothes was injured and taken to the Infirmary.' Perhaps the estimate of fifty was exaggerated as there were only nine arrests in the end, but the episode shows how little the gangs feared the police. No names were given in the article.

On 7 September *The Times* reported further trouble. Harry Sabini, invariably described at this time as a 'fruit dealer', was in court charged with threatening Fred Gilbert with an automatic pistol at Paddington Station on a train bound for Bath races. Gilbert was brought to the court from his cell as he was already on remand on another offence for reasons described below. Gilbert said that 'he had taken his seat in a race train going to Bath when the prisoner and several other men came to the carriage door, and Sabini, presenting a pistol at him, said, "I will blow your brains out". The witness called a policeman, and as he did so all the men ran away.'

Gilbert admitted to being a former member of the Bookmakers' Protection Association but he said they discharged him after he was attacked by the Sabini gang which 'caused him to have sixty-two stitches put in his leg, five in his face, and four in the back of his head'. Whether he was discharged for being incompetent or for getting too involved in the Sabini feud is not clarified.

In *The Times* of 11 September 1922 we discover that Fred Gilbert and George 'Brummie' Sage are up to their old tricks, this time alongside Fred Brett. They were committed for trial at the Old Bailey charged with 'demanding £10 with menaces from Harry Margulas, clerk'. All three denied the allegation. Margulas claimed that Gilbert and Brett had accosted him in Claremont Square, waved a revolver in his face and demanded £10. A similar event occurred at Nottingham two weeks later when he was stopped again by Gilbert and Brett and 'five or six others' demanding ten pounds with a revolver. When the two caught up with Margulas again a week later, in a pub near Waterloo Station, a demand was again made for £10, with Gilbert using a gun and Brett a carving knife to emphasize their threat. The claim for ten pounds seems to have originated from an unpaid gambling debt. There is an implication that Margulas was connected with the Sabini gang as he denied in court that Darby Sabini was the head of a racing gang, despite him being one of the most notorious gang leaders of his time.

In November the plot thickened. Four men, including Fred Gilbert's brother John, were acquitted on the charge of conspiring to persuade Harry Margulas to give false evidence at the trial, presumably to induce him to claim that the others had not demanded money with menaces. In the end everyone was acquitted of all charges, whether trying to extort money or inducing others to pervert the course of justice. It is easy to see how difficult it was to prosecute individual slices of offending in a gang feud when so many people were trying to muddy the waters and threaten witnesses.

The following day, another *Times* article detailed an altercation in the Chatfields Hotel in Brighton, where a large number of racegoers were present. George Langham and James Ford were committed for trial for causing grievous bodily harm to John Thomas Phillips by slashing his face with a razor and kicking and punching him. During the hearing Langham announced that his real name was Angelo Gianicoli and that he 'shouted the numbers' for the Bookmakers' Protection Association. He also admitted to knowing Alf White, of whom more below, who was awaiting trial for shooting with intent to murder. These complex, interwoven brawls and violent disagreements were difficult for the courts to unravel and seemed to be increasing in frequency.

A lengthy feud was in prospect. On 4 November 1922 a longer piece appeared in *The Times* about two violent altercations. A total of seven men were being sentenced that day. Three were guilty of the attempted shooting of a police officer near Gray's Inn Road. Four others, including Joseph Sabini, were guilty of offences in connection with another shooting affray in Mornington Crescent. Sabini himself got three years' penal servitude, with witnesses laughably trying to dissociate him from the notorious Sabini gang. Another name stands out: Alfred White, who was given five years' penal servitude. White had been a steward of the controversial Bookmakers' Protection Association, which was an attempt by the Jockey Club to provide professional security at racecourses but in reality it was staffed with violent gang members. The complicated web of networks in horse racing at that time led to a Jockey Club official and former Chief Inspector Divall, now of the Jockey Club, testifying to White's good character. There was sometimes evidence that witnesses speaking up in defence of gang members were themselves involved, often receiving money for their trouble. Mr Justice Roche remained clear-eyed: 'I am not going to investigate the merits or demerits of the Bookmakers'

Protection Association.' He later added that White was lucky not to have been up on a capital charge, indicating that the perpetrators of the Mornington Crescent shooting narrowly avoided anyone being killed.

On 21 November 1922 Harry Sabini was shot in the abdomen and taken to the Royal Free Hospital. Other sources suggest that Harry and Charles 'Darby' Sabini had gone to the Fratellanza Club in Clerkenwell to meet the Cortesi brothers to negotiate a bigger share of racecourse takings. The Cortesis had recently switched allegiance to the Gilberts and George Sage, allied with the Birmingham gang. Two of the Cortesis were eventually sent to prison for the shooting, helping the Sabinis gain influence in their absence.

By June 1925 the truce between the London and Birmingham race gangs was truly over. The *Daily Mirror* reported a vicious fight near Piccadilly in London which started at two o'clock in the morning after London gang members waited outside a nightclub for the Birmingham gang to emerge. The usual weapons were used, causing minor head injuries. The police turned up quickly and dispersed the fighters. The injured men were led away by friends, so nobody was treated in hospital.

Just a few days later, six men were remanded in custody, this time in Birmingham, for badly slashing a known Birmingham gang member with a razor. The prosecuting solicitor claimed that Thomas MacDonald's face was 'slit from ear to lip'. The paper claims that, had the assailants not been arrested there and then, a mass brawl would have started. The same case was serious enough to receive coverage as far away as the *Fermanagh Times* in Northern Ireland. The paper suggests that Thomas MacDonald also went by the name McDonagh. Both names tend to indicate an Irish background. This time the word was that the victim had been 'slit from the top to the bottom of his face with a razor'.

In August 1925 the *Birmingham Gazette* blamed the violence, of which Birmingham remained 'comparatively free', on visiting London gang members travelling with the express intent of carrying out reprisals on Birmingham members. Seemingly unaware of the logical conclusion that implied the Birmingham members had been causing trouble in

London, as shown in the accounts of June 1925 above, the paper suggests that a recent case involving a slashing was not proceeded with because the victim refused to give evidence against the perpetrators, another hallmark of gang behaviour that made prosecutions less frequent than they would otherwise have been.

Although the 1920s is remembered as the zenith of the horse racing gangs, problems continued to emerge after the Second World War. Just before Christmas 1946, the *London News Chronicle* reports that representatives of several unnamed gangs had been summoned to Scotland Yard for a meeting. This is extraordinary because it shows that the police acknowledged the gangs and the severity of the problem they caused, but also their powerlessness, because the purpose of the meeting was to agree a verbal truce only. Nobody was arrested and no weapons were confiscated. 'It was to have been the bloodiest mob warfare this country had ever known. Razors, coshes, and iron tubes encased in rubber would have been the least of the weapons. Revolvers, Sten guns and hand grenades were the mobsters' armaments.' The police had received prior information about a planned battle and were working proactively to stop it. This is the only mention of hand grenades I have seen and might reflect the illicit flow of military-grade wartime weapons into the hands of private gangs. This article is explicitly tied to the racecourse gangs and explains their preferred business model of threatening bookmakers with violence if they did not pay out protection money. This 'service' was also offered to nightclub owners, reinforcing the fact that the racecourse gangs operated widely in other areas of organized crime. One intriguing aspect is that one of the terms of the truce was that an injured gang member be offered compensation, presumably from the gang that attacked him: 'One of the terms of the peace treaty has been the offer of several thousands of pounds to a gangster injured in a gang battle last week. This man was injured so severely when he followed his leader into their rival's territory that he had to be taken to hospital.' He was still in hospital a week later.

Although the horse racing gangs grabbed most of the headlines throughout the postwar period, *The Times* of 17 November 1936 reported ugly scenes from Wandsworth Greyhound Stadium in which a man had been stabbed and killed. Bert Marsh and Herbert Wilkins were charged with the murder of Massimino Monte-Columbo and of wounding Massimino's brother Camillo with intent to murder. All four men were employed by the stadium but were also mixed up in gang activity. A life preserver was found at the scene and there were suggestions that a bar stool had been used as a weapon.

By the end of 1949 the gang violence at the racecourses was dimming in the memory, but the press were still vigilant. This time, the *Evening Despatch* of 16 December 1949 is worrying about the doping of horses, stating that '20 trainers have had their licences withdrawn during the past two years because horses in their charge have been found to be doped'. Although the trainers were punished according to the rules, the article claims that they were not the culprits, and that racing gangs were administering dope to certain horses during short periods when the horses were unsupervised, either to speed them up or slow them down. The article claims to know of one such ringleader, a 'one-time greyhound owner [who] owns a number of shops and an attractive house' and two former pickpocket friends who together made over £100,000 in the previous year, an amount equivalent to around £4 million today. It was big business without much skill or finesse needed and it is suggested that similar activities were carried on in Birmingham, Newmarket and Epsom, among other places. These crimes could be accomplished without the need for physical violence or threats, and a careful doper was difficult to catch, needing only a few seconds with a horse to inject the drug.

Chapter 4

Gambling, Boxing and Burglary

One way of tracking gangs and organized crime through the decades and centuries is to look at their evolving business models. The phrase 'business model' might feel modern, but the idea of building up a set of products or services is just as important in organized crime as it is in legitimate business, even if the plans arise more by instinct and custom than deep analysis of alternatives.

Another feature of the times we are looking at are the American and British temperance movements. Only America banned alcohol outright during the prohibition years but there was still a temperance movement in Britain that led to shops which looked outwardly like pubs serving only carbonated drinks such as Dandelion and Burdock. And it was prohibition that provided the most important early business model for the American Mafia. Banning alcohol did not remove people's fondness for drinking it. The whole industry was forced underground, where gangs could get good money for providing even the poorest quality homemade 'moonshine' drinks. The early famous gangsters like Al Capone, whom we will meet in the chapter on America, used the prohibition of alcohol to create a lucrative and violent business.

Before getting into violent crime and its other possible business models, we should consider whether there are easier, safer ways to make quick money illegally. Enter the long con trick.

Easy Fraud: The Long Con

I found Charles Kingston's brilliant 1924 study of British criminals, *A Gallery of Rogues*, hiding at the back of a second-hand bookshop.

Kingston devotes a whole chapter to 'rogues of the turf' and considers that there were many successful frauds associated with horse racing that required no strongmen, threats, or actual violence. Of all the gambling options then and now, horse racing is the most popular. Thousands of rational, logical punters leave their wits at the door when they embark on a day at the races. There is an addictive ambience on a bright summer day when the Pimms is flowing freely, and the bookmakers scream their odds, ratcheting up the suspense and excitement. A sizeable minority will believe any story, and this romantic disregard for common sense could be taken advantage of.

Kingston's first and most successful rogue of the turf was George Hunt, of Barry in Wales. Hunt was so successful, beyond his dreams, that the sheer amount of cash sent to him became a problem in itself. Half a million pounds found its way to his modest house in a short time. Thousands responded to his finely crafted circular promising anyone an incredible ten per cent a week interest on any amount they cared to send him. It wasn't only the punters who were taken in. An unnamed bookmaker sent £500 to Hunt. All kinds of professional people, including lawyers and bank managers, and people from the working classes fell for Hunt's simple letter. There is no totally scientific way to map half a million pounds in 1922 to today's money, but one reliable source suggests it might be worth over £30 million. Whichever multiplier you choose, it is an eye-watering sum bearing in mind that the 'investors' sent this money to someone they had never met, based only on a letter. Hunt was caught and sentenced to three years' penal servitude, defending his method of picking winners at the racetrack to the last. It started to look like sending men to the racecourse to threaten bookmakers face-to-face was a poor alternative to such a low risk, surefire scheme as George Hunt's.

These schemes were not unique to Britain. Kingston relates another story involving Max Klante of Berlin, who lured even more money, millions of pounds, from German pockets at Karlshorst races. Klante seems to have been the Bernie Madoff of the early 1920s, soliciting over

12 million marks and attaining notoriety. A truly lovable rogue, he was hiding in plain sight as he swindled tens of thousands of victims. He disappeared when a prominent Berlin lawyer, who had invested a million of his own money in the Ponzi scheme, asked to see the accounts in detail.

A more complex case involved the Bank of Liverpool itself. A corrupt clerk at the bank, Thomas Goudie, stole £168,000 over a four-year period yet did not profit himself from his crime. The sum was so great that the bank's dividend for 1902 was reduced from 10 to 8 per cent and the bank had to tighten its security procedures. Closer investigation revealed that Goudie was stealing the money to pay blackmailers who were members of a gang working the racecourse. Although he had started off stealing money to bet on his own account, he was spotted by the blackmailers at Hurst Park races in West Molesey, Surrey. The course was also known for an arson attack staged by suffragettes in revenge for the death of Emily Davison at Epsom in 1913. Goudie attracted the wrong sort of attention by betting in large notes and was approached by a gang member who promised him dead cert tips. The depths of Goudie's gullibility ran deep and he sent the tipster £25,000 within two weeks. Goudie was not familiar with the intricacies of gambling at the racecourse and believed that there was no limit to the sums that could be staked. The gang members simply picked the most unlikely horses to bet on, although no bets were ever placed, the bets would always lose, and they pocketed Goudie's stake every time. There was only one tight moment in the gang's otherwise foolproof scheme. Every so often, as in a lottery, a rank outsider will win a race. Goudie had provided the gang with £30,000 to stake on such a horse and, when it won, he realized he would be able to repay every penny he stole from his employer, the Bank of Liverpool, and still have enough for a comfortable retirement. The gang had already divided his £30,000 in the certain belief that the horse would lose. It is not difficult to imagine Goudie's shock when he received a letter informing him that, at the last moment, his tipster had changed his mind and bet on a different horse that he felt was more likely to win than the one he had mentioned to Thomas Goudie. Whenever

Goudie got cold feet, the gang threatened to expose his fraud and get him fired from the bank. Eventually, Goudie and four members of the tipster gang were caught and charged. In a final injustice, Goudie was the only member of the ring to die in prison, at Parkhurst.

These stories of the gullible nature of gamblers suggest that making money illegitimately was much easier than beating up bookmakers at the racecourse. But they all have one thing in common: all the perpetrators were caught and sent to prison for long stretches. It also takes a particular blend of arrogance and imagination to actually consider that such transparent ruses could work. Whatever the answer, Billy Kimber, the Sabinis and others preferred more physical methods to extract money. In this way, they could keep their own hands clean, such that others would be arrested and imprisoned if things went wrong.

The Short Con

There were less elaborate ruses deployed in the street on gullible members of the public all the time. We should make a distinction between the violence of the professional racing gangs and the short street altercation in which violence plays no part. Although victims will feel foolish and are financially harmed from these transparent tricks, they are not terrified in the process, and the tricks are just as easily carried out by a lone operator as by an organized group.

The *Sunday Sun* had two such examples in August 1921 which it put under the headline 'Gang of Tricksters', yet the gang angle is not proven. As a female customer left a bank in London's West End with some cash she had just withdrawn, she was approached by a man pretending to be a clerk at the bank. He asked her to accept an envelope in exchange for the money she had just drawn out and disappeared after they had made the exchange. When the customer opened the envelope she found it to be empty. The most telling detail the newspaper could muster up about the perpetrator was that the man was 'hatless', a sign of the times.

A male American tourist was approached in the same week by two men he did not know. They entrusted him with a watch that appeared to be gold and disappeared. When they returned, the tourist returned the watch and they requested that he show similar trust in themselves. He gave them £16 in notes and they disappeared, never to return.

Apart from the transparent and rudimentary nature of these cons, what they have in common is that the perpetrators targeted the vulnerable or people lacking in confidence to increase their chance of success. The young woman outside the bank, already nervous perhaps to be carrying cash, and the American tourist, too disoriented to spot the trick. Tourists always seem to be too trusting of the local population. But would these constitute gang crime in the common understanding? Not from today's perspective where we would see the perpetrators as con artists rather than a threat to public safety.

Cheque Fraud

The *North Mail and Newcastle Chronicle* of 20 December 1927 documents a number of frauds designed to make money for gang members. The main case, for which four men were sent to prison, involved the stealing of letters that had been dropped into post-boxes. If the thieves found a letter with a cheque inside, they would steal the cheque and use the details to open an account at the victim's bank, forging the signature they copied from the letter. Once the thieves had obtained a pristine new chequebook from the bank, they could write cheques in the name of the victim at will. The banks were lax in not checking the details of the possessor of any cheque, and the perpetrators had successfully pulled off this trick a number of times.

One of the defendants, Benjamin Harper, turns out to have been a career criminal after he left the army as an acting captain. He had been living on his wits as a racing tipster. He had been an associate of Josephine O'Dare, of whom more later, recently convicted of a series of forgeries, and was suspected of human trafficking.

Another defendant that day, John Francis O'Connor, had nine convictions against him in the English courts and was also considered a criminal in France. He had been involved in smuggling white slaves between France and England. O'Connor had a particularly ingenious fraud to his name. He had posed as someone who could feed legitimate French news stories to the English press in London. He sent one legitimate story to establish his credentials, and then, using the false name of Frank Stewart, sent a fake story about himself being involved in the murder of a nurse. One London paper unquestioningly published this fake story, enabling John O'Connor to sue the paper for libel. Only a detailed investigation by the newspaper's lawyer uncovered O'Connor's deception and he was arrested.

The group was enabled by Luke Donegal, a skilled artist who had forged documents before. The documents could be used as references, in one case for obtaining a luxury apartment. This forgery ring could only have been carried out by a gang due to the different skills required. Stealing the letters, then confidently and calmly presenting the cheques at banks, and artistically forging documents, were skills unlikely to be found in a single individual. The level of creativity involved in thinking up the steps of the frauds, as well as copying documents when needed, took real skill. So although these crimes were not violent, and should have been lucrative, some small detail tripped the gang up each time. There was no foolproof method of raising money that could be reliably repeated. One way to evade capture would be to try the same fraud in different parts of the country, so that the local police would not be wise to whatever ruse was in play, but such mobility would have been beyond many at that time.

Boxing and other sports

Several sources mention horse racing and boxing as being important sports in the lives of the gangs. As Charles Kingston said, 'At that time there was a certain gang of needy hangers-on of the turf and the

boxing ring, men who lived from hand to mouth and endured all sorts
of discomforts in order that they might avoid honest work.' Fighting
on the streets was made easier if you knew how to handle yourself in
the ring, which in turn gave fighting skills a semi-legitimate outlet and
a way to gamble at the same time.

In Fulham, West London 7 November 1952 was a busy day. According
to the *Fulham Chronicle* eight boys had been caught stealing cash from
buses that were parked outside the Empress Hall in Earl's Court. It stood
where the Empress State Building stands today, near West Brompton
underground station. The boys were fined between 5 and 15 shillings,
explicitly to be paid out of their own pocket money over a period of weeks.
The paper also reported a wedding at All Saints' Church, Fulham, for
which the bride's father made the two-tier wedding cake. This was all
on the same page as the news that the MP for West Fulham, Dr Edith
Summerskill, was blaming boxing as the root of crime. An article
reported a long speech on the occasion of the opening of a 'mothercraft'
conference at Central Hall, Westminster. Dr Summerskill asked why so
much attention was given to young children who were then neglected
in adolescence. In just one year, 100,000 men had been convicted of
offences, of whom 40,000 were under 21. Dr Summerskill indirectly
blamed their mothers. The Queen herself had refused to be a patron
of the Boxing Association, Dr Summerskill went on. Dr Summerskill's
claims could be balanced close to home. Her opponent for the seat of
West Fulham, Mrs Mabel de la Motte, Conservative, was a vice president
of West Ham boxing club and also vice president of the Fulham Amateur
Boxing Club. Mrs de la Motte claimed that Dr Summerskill could not
give even one example of a 'cosh boy' who was involved in any amateur
boxing club.

Our distance from the immediate post-war period, and the weight
of research accumulated by those such as John Barron Mays, suggests
that Mrs de la Motte is closer to the truth. A reader's letter from Frank
Gefford, a member of the boxing referees' association, published on
14 November in the *Fulham Chronicle*, rubbishes Dr Summerskill's

views. He asks readers whether the Oxford and Cambridge University boxing clubs, or the boxing clubs organized for staff at hospitals or other places of work, were really training hoodlums. Frank Gefford would presumably agree that boys' clubs, including boxing clubs, which sought to organize activities for bored and energetic young men, were part of the solution to crime, not a cause. Whether or not this random day in Fulham in 1952 represents a pattern is left to the reader to consider. But this random page in a local newspaper shows a country in flux. Men were baking cakes, as described on the same page in the article 'Bride's father made the cake', naughty boys were being dealt with gently by the justice system, and boxing was being cited as both the cause and the cure for a perceived glut in violent young men.

An article from 1906 in Coleshill, Birmingham, suggests that any event drawing a large crowd could be subject to small-time gambling cons, not just boxing or horse racing. The *Coleshill Chronicle* of Saturday, 16 June, describes a game of 'over and under' that turned to violence when the police got involved. This is a dice game in which punters bet a small wager as to whether the combined score of the dice thrown by the organizer will be higher or lower than some number. On this occasion the dice were thrown onto a sheet marked out with numbers, calling to mind a rudimentary version of roulette. The pure version of the game involving only dice was ripe for abuse simply by using loaded dice. The game would always be rigged in favour of the man running the stall.

The game was being played at a track and field athletics event and the *Chronicle* made the unsubstantiated claim that it was a commonplace occurrence at athletics events. On this day, it was at the sports ground of the Rudge-Whitworth manufacturing company. The crowd of punters would each commit small stakes of a few pennies. William Williams was the offender on this occasion and drew attention by how he responded to the policeman trying to break up the game. A rumour went around that police were in the area, so Williams stopped the game and rolled up his sheet, then others turned on him and said he should be arrested for gambling. Williams was cornered and began attacking Detective

Sergeant Bassett. An associate of Williams, most likely James Gill, managed to spirit away the evidence of the sheet as other police officers arrived. The crowd must have been considerable (the paper claiming thirty or forty) because it was difficult for Bassett to remove Williams from the scene.

Organizing a game was an offence but playing the game was not, so without the sheet Williams was free to admit to being just one of many punters playing for fun. Unfortunately, witnesses came forward who saw Williams attacking the police officer. The police stated that the organizers of these games came to the city in gangs and were a persistent pest. When found guilty on both charges, a long list of prior convictions of Williams was announced. Williams was given a heavy fine of twenty shillings or a month in prison if he could not find the money.

This episode shows how prevalent small-time gambling operations were at this time, even away from the headline-grabbing sports of horse racing and boxing. It seems that any crowd at a sports event or fair carried the opportunity to make a few shillings, and many individuals took advantage; although they were not the well-organized violent gangs involved in shooting and slashing bookmakers, they would undoubtedly be labelled anti-social today, not least for their quick resort to fighting whenever the police stepped in.

Countryside Options

To close this chapter, let us briefly consider the extent of organized crime in the countryside. If we understand the main drivers to be poverty, having too much time available at weekends with too little options to fill the hours, and a culture where teenagers did not attend school, then we should find gang behaviour prevalent in rural areas too. But we do not.

There are other drivers at work that lead to the formation of violent gangs. One of these must surely be the sense of victim anonymity: you cannot beat up someone you know because they will identify you to the police. Only another gang member would stop short of grassing, to protect himself and the unwritten gang honour. To a gang member, police officers are a more steadfast enemy than any other rival gang.

It seems that the delicate gang ecosystem never got started in the countryside. Gangs did not develop because there were no other gangs to fight against. One reason for this is that there were too few people from whom to recruit, and only a tiny minority of any population ever got moved to join a gang and follow that way of life, even for their teenage years.

There was crime in the countryside, of course, but the social bonds of rural life were stronger. There were few dark alleys to melt into. Not only did everyone know everyone, but they had lived in the same small towns and villages for generations. You would know everyone's parents and grandparents, and they would live a short walk away. There were far fewer people migrating into the villages bringing new ideas and weakening the traditions. As we know, hundreds of thousands of people were moving in the opposite direction, towards the cities, in search of better paid work. The crisis of declining populations we see in today's villages began a century ago, when young people were unable to resist the lure of the city of the industrial revolution. They never returned and neither did their children.

Some of the crimes which were carried on in the countryside include horse nobbling and cattle smuggling, but poaching is an obvious option that was not present in the cities. On 29 August 1903 the *Newcastle Chronicle* has an in-depth column and a half on the methods used by partridge poaching gangs to outwit the landowners, gamekeepers and even the police, who had recently been instructed to round up anyone loitering in the countryside without good reason. The poaching gangs sent individual spies roaming across fields, pretending to look for mushrooms and herbs. The spies are looking for evidence of where partridges 'juck' or sleep overnight and listening out for the sounds of the cock partridge calling out to nearby hens. The partridges stand in a circle, tails outmost, heads to the wind so they can listen for intruders. Spending their nights on the ground protects partridges from the dangers of the forest, where the prey of other birds roams freely. But it also exposes them to poaching gangs, wise to the ways of the partridge, who come with large nets and scoop up whole groups of them in one swoop. To stop the nets, the landowners arrange for open fields to be arrayed with thorns which snag the nets and cause delay and frustration to would-be poachers.

If the nets seem a little too prosaic, there are two other methods described in this engaging article. One is to get the partridges disoriented by soaking seed in rum and casting it across the field. After the partridges greedily gobble the food, they begin staggering around and can easily be captured. If both nets and alcohol seem a little one-sided, the final, and amazingly creative, method, is to attach a candle around the neck of a patient dog. As the dog wanders around the field, looking for partridge, the poachers follow behind. When the partridges see the unexpected light they stand totally still and can easily be rounded up by the poachers.

These activities were played out year after year and required several people, including the spies, and the poachers holding the nets, to be successful. It is non-violent to humans, of course, but this is one way the countryside can support organized crime of its own. The loss of game from a landowner's fields and woods is every bit as economically painful as thieving would be from shops and homes in the city, but this is not the typical habitat we imagine when thinking of pre-war gang life.

Poaching was not constrained to field game either. In June 1948, the *Kentish Express* reported that organized gangs were stealing fish in Kent and East Sussex. They used cars to travel to and from London. Their usual method of stealing the fish was to use a 'stop and sleeve net' after first 'bumping the water' to encourage fish into the net. Fish, including boxes of tench, bream, rudd and roach, were stolen. The newspaper is just as indignant that the poaching was carried on outside the fishing season.

Chapter 5

Provincial Gangs: England

This chapter ventures beyond London, to England's largest cities at a time when they were growing fast due to increased industrialization. People moved to the great cities in huge numbers for more reliable work with good pay. Why then did a significant minority of younger lads organize themselves into gangs?

Birmingham

Birmingham has received attention for its inter-war gangs in recent years thanks to the BBC series *Peaky Blinders*. The gangs thrived in large industrial cities, and Birmingham was second only to London in size and industry. It had a local coal supply and a fabulous canal network that could transport steel anywhere in Britain and beyond to the British Empire. It was an exhilarating and terrifying place to live at a unique point in the city's history.

January 1904 and gang trouble is coming once more. The *Birmingham Daily Mail* fretted that the old 'slogger' gangs had returned to Birmingham. The police had said in Old Hill Police Court that 'the Black Country "hooligan" or "slogger" still survives but, happily, in a form very modified from that he assumed years ago, when the notorious Smethwick Black Gang was the terror of the district, and almost the despair of local police'. Another culprit known as the Aston Slogger was mentioned, which also refers to a local gang. The members of these gangs ranged in age from 16 to 23. However, the size of the gangs must have made them a terrifying sight. 'A gang was usually about twenty or thirty strong, and the members were armed with stout sticks, handkerchiefs in which stones were fastened, and buckled belts. On rare occasions knives were used.' This article is notable for its early date, coming over a decade before the heyday of the more famous Peaky Blinders, and also for some of the details. No mention of guns, and knives used only rarely. But the article also points out something that many modern observers overlook: the gangs did not restrict their violence only towards other gangs. Any member of the public in the wrong place at the wrong time could be singled out once the adrenalin rushed. Even more surprising is a note about women getting stuck into the fighting, although not usually declared in the press as gang members in their own right. A final striking observation is made that is worth keeping in mind throughout this book: 'There is, however, a good deal of worldly wisdom in the old saying, "Give a dog a bad name and you may as well hang him".' Yes, the word gang or slogger, the identification of the group as the criminal actor, tended to dehumanize the gang members, for which in the public eye no punishment was severe enough. These boys knew that if someone was accidentally killed in one of their fights, they would hang for it. They chose their weapons carefully with this possibility in mind, using knives rarely and even then in a careful way designed to cause painful injuries but not death.

This article sets the tone for the early part of the twentieth century in Birmingham. It is an editorial piece, not reporting a specific court case, but the key elements of gang activity that would later become notorious are noted here. No glamour or honour among gangs is mentioned. The gangs, although staffed by very young men and teenaged boys, were a menace to be stamped out.

The end of 1904 brought the retirement from the Aston Police of Detective Sergeant Whitcroft, an event noted in the *Birmingham Daily News*. One of three vivid memories recounted by Whitcroft at this time were his days working against two Birmingham slogging gangs: the Ten Arches Gang and the Whitehouse Street Gang, both reported as no longer active in 1904. Whitcroft remembers the weapons used by those gangs: 'they were armed with buckled belts, life preservers, iron tubes into the end of which molten lead had been run.' The life preserver was also known as the cosh and was designed to stun the victim without causing serious injury. This weapon appears in news articles across the country, showing again how keen the gangs were to avoid irreparable harm to their victims, at least during these early years of the new century.

October 1905 brought the news that Frederick Timbrell, a man shot five days previously in a Saturday night affray, had died of his injuries. This was the result of a feud. The man accused of shooting Timbrell, William Lacey, had previously attacked Timbrell by biting his ear. The shooting had been preceded by a drinking session in the aptly named Robin Hood pub in Summer Hill Street. Trouble started when two other men, Scott and Casey, began a fistfight. During their fight, a shot rang out, and Timbrell fell to the ground injured. The weapon was never discovered. The newspaper, the *Birmingham Gazette and Express*, makes plain the effect this news had on the perpetrator, William Lacey. He was reported to faint more than once on hearing the news of his victim's death. He was under no illusion that he would hang for his crime in all probability. If Lacey had possessed the forethought to imagine this reaction *prior* to shooting another man dead, it is unlikely he would have carried out his action. An inability to imagine future consequences is one of the many reasons that prison, even the death penalty, did not seem to deter many gang members. They mainly went out of their way to avoid outright murder but, in the heat of battle, other urges took over. The one mitigation in favour of Lacey is that Timbrell was believed to be in possession of a knife and, given their previous history, Lacey may well have considered himself the target of Timbrell's blade. The newspaper imagines other defences for Lacey: perhaps he did not intend to pull the trigger, or perhaps he intended to fire into the air. Perhaps Lacey did not realize the safety catch was off or that the gun was loaded, and no doubt all of these defences had been used before. Either way, the paper is clear that this was a fight between gang members and that many others not identified by police were involved in the affray that Saturday evening.

It was December before Lacey's fate became known. Charged with murder at the Birmingham Assizes, the jury found him guilty only of manslaughter and he was sentenced to seven years' penal servitude, equivalent to imprisonment with hard labour. The short paragraph announcing this news two days before Christmas 1905 is also notable for calling the two men 'Brummagem Savages', a label which has stood the test of time to describe the various Birmingham gangs. This article has no doubt that the men were members of rival gangs and this was a gang-on-gang matter. But the fatal use of a revolver remained rare.

Three men were found guilty of the attempted murder of Samuel Sheldon on 7 December 1912, and a fourth man guilty of causing bodily harm. They received sentences from two years to ten years with hard labour. The headline is 'Dangerous Birmingham Gang'. This one stands out for its brevity. Had gang violence become routine? We know that shootings were rare, so why wasn't this event captured in more detail? The offenders are not named and the name of their gang is not given, if there was one. Perhaps the newspaper title gives us a clue: the *Westminster Gazette*. Birmingham gang trouble seems to have become national-level news, even rating a mention in London which had its own gang troubles. However, another London paper adds a small but important detail: 'The quarrel arose out of what was known as the Garrison Lane Vendetta, in connection with which several other men are serving sentences of penal servitude. Sheldon was a member of the rival gang.'

Use of a pistol provoked the long sentences, with Charles Franklin receiving the ten-year sentence, most likely indicating him to be the trigger man. The Garrison Lane Vendetta is one of the signal events in the lore of the *Peaky Blinders*' series, and that area of Birmingham was where the fictional Shelby brothers made their headquarters.

Manchester

Ancoats, Manchester. The Ancoats of 1890 is still recognizable in the Ancoats of today. The mills are still there, the canals are still there. Back then, poverty meant shared water taps and toilets, and disease. Today, the poor housing has in places been replaced with luxury apartments, not in those long-demolished back-to-back terraced houses, but within the old mills themselves, with their gigantic windows and bare brickwork. The best buildings back then were the mills and factories, with vast spaces and high ceilings which today make excellent apartments and offices. Within the old brickwork, Ancoats has gone upmarket.

In Manchester, fights between gangs, or groups of youths at any rate, became known as scuttling. The lads who did the fighting, often armed with anything short of guns, were known as scuttlers. Although Manchester had its own name for these fights, the weapons are familiar from other places. Knives were routine, but not the most eye-catching of weapons. Pokers were used, even cutlasses, getting more exotic. There were sticks with lead in the ends, and pieces of leather with iron hardware like bolts attached. The most mundane of the weapons, other than fists, were stones and belts. In short, anything that came to hand in an industrial city teeming with factory workers, could become a weapon. Sometimes the factory equipment itself was used to manufacture iron weapons. The belt buckles were very large and heavy. Made of brass, they might be three inches across. Such a belt, when wielded by a determined scuttler, could crack a human skull.

Andrew Davies' excellent book *The Gangs of Manchester* mentions a local journalist, Alexander Devine, who chronicled the gangs of Manchester and Salford. He believed there were four causes of gang violence. First there were the parents. Weak, absent parents fostered an environment of neglect and indiscipline within the home. One of the many complexities of studying the gangs at this distance are the contradictions. At the time, welfare organizations had become established to help alleviate poverty. Could the existence of welfare, coming from outside the home, have undermined the parents? One of these organizations was the NSPCC, still at the forefront of child protection today. Devine then turned his ire on the schools. Weakness began in the home, but the schools and teachers were to blame also. The context for this is that school became compulsory between the ages of five and ten in 1880. This gave children a place and a purpose but did not manage to improve the behaviour of the most violent youths, the lads who would scuttle in the streets. Although these times are commonly associated with corporal punishment, the cane was restricted to the more expensive schools. Working class boys were not physically punished, and the newspapers of the time often complained that the scuttlers were not subjected to corporal punishment either. Devine himself was an advocate for corporal punishment, believing that discipline would only come if it was backed up by violence. Devine reminds us that this belief was common at the time. Third, the reading material of the working class was to blame for the unruly fights. This was the age of the penny-dreadful story, the Netflix of its day. Cheap to buy, serialized works with cliff-hangers, violence and gore, there was a lot of blood. The lads lapped them up and passed them around. And finally, in Devine's assessment of the Manchester crime problem, was sheer boredom. Long, hard days at work were followed by empty evenings with nothing to do and nowhere to go.

We can look at Devine's beliefs with confident scepticism now, a century after he was writing about the gangs of the north-west. But is there something to his fourth and final claim: that boredom contributes to petty crime, which in itself is one of the symptoms of poverty. Without money, there was nothing to do after work. If your father and elder brothers take to hitting their friends in mass brawls once a week, it seems highly likely that a younger and more impressionable brother would follow their example. Could it be as simple as that?

As the twentieth century beckoned, with all its new ideas about global war and destruction, scuttling and the Manchester gangs declined. As we have found throughout this book, the reasons behind any trend are many and varied. Even before the Great War of 1914 loomed, there was the South African Boer War, a rehearsal, in hindsight. The physical qualities of men available for fighting were an international embarrassment. According to Andrew Davies, of the 12,000 confident, proud souls who signed up for Boer action, fully 8,000 were completely rejected as unfit and only around a thousand were declared fully fit to fight. These formerly terrifying scuttlers were brave, but not so frightening any more. Even worse, these problems were not confined to the north-west. The issues were similar in Birmingham, Liverpool, London and beyond to Scotland and Ireland too. These issues could not be blamed on individual depredation any longer: if a majority of British men were too weak to fight, it spoke of larger societal problems in the cities, and the tide of public opinion began to turn.

Matters were so urgent that in the Bengal Street area of Ancoats, 239 houses were immediately marked for demolition, affecting over a thousand individuals. In its place came Victoria Square, a block of almost three hundred flats that would house these families in comparative luxury. The Victorian age which had spawned so many filthy chimneys was now repaying the workers with new homes.

Perhaps the buildings were top priority because they were the most visible problem. If so, health and morality were not far behind. Again, the chimneys and factories could be blamed for the environmental health of Manchester and Salford's occupants. The deeper you dig into the problems of the Victorian inner cities, the more often you see that the problems were mainly by-products of rapid industrialization. The Victorian capitalists put money before health, and only addressed health when the money was at risk. They were a more extreme version of the twenty-first century capitalist: the spectrum nudges forwards but the attitudes can be easily compared. The dawn of the temperance era can be seen in hindsight too. Yes, the air was full of toxic gas, the sewers and toilets were inadequate, but it could not be escaped that there were rather a high number of pubs and bottle shops too.

Amongst the gang members, and even before the wars grabbed mainstream attention, life was improved by the lads' clubs, sometimes organised by factory management and other times by local churches. Alexander Devine was an advocate for creating more lads' clubs. For men and boys with jobs, poverty was not so easy to blame for gang violence. Perhaps evening boredom was involved, too? The working day in the factory started and finished earlier than the modern nine-to-five office day, and who could blame the men for marauding around the streets after dark? Promoting activity clubs for the younger men also contributed to a fall in crime and violence in this period. Davies again highlights an example provided by former journalist Devine at this time. As a *Manchester Guardian* court reporter, Devine had seen the depravity virtually first-hand as these terrorists paraded through the city's court system. He quickly realized that the lads themselves were actually victims of a poor society, and in just three months the lads' club he established in Mulberry Street had seven hundred regular members. If the gangs had been frightening, they had never been able to boast such weight of numbers. It turned out to be true: the lads were bored as well as poor, but they were not inherently bad. As soon as an alternative lifestyle was provided, they jumped at the chance. From these early beginnings, the current broad reach of after-school clubs can be seen: Scouts, Guides, and all the related brigades and movements can be dated back to these decades at the turn of the twentieth century.

By the 1890s and into the new century, Charles Russell took up the cause of the lads' clubs. In 1892, Russell moved to Manchester just as Devine left the city. Russell worked for the London and North Western Railway, and began to volunteer at a local lads' club, founding a company of the Boys' Brigade in 1893. Although the numbers of children involved seems impressive from this standpoint, Russell himself was reluctant to boast. It turned out that the lads who flocked to the clubs were not quite the most violent, but a couple of steps up. Russell suggested that the roughest lads were actually the hardest to sign up and retain. But Davies seems to strike the right balance: he suggests that although direct membership of the poorest and most violent lads might have been low in proportion to the population overall, the influence of the clubs was dramatic in society at large. We can see that this is so, over a century later. We can see that the health problems in Britain almost lost the Boer War. And once the factory owners started to see a risk to their profits, down came the slums, the lads' clubs began, and gang membership dwindled. This did not happen suddenly, and not as neatly as it might look. But over the decades leading up to the Great War, British youths, men in particular, became fitter, less poor and less violent. And this was also the time when football rose to prominence, with the English FA being formed in 1863. Gradually, but irrevocably, boys had wider choices about how to spend their expanding leisure time.

If the causes of gang violence in general, and the Manchester and Salford scuttlers in particular, were varied and complex, so were the reasons for its demise. There is some evidence that harsher court sentences were not dissuasive. The magistrates were denied their wish to have gang members flogged, however. Yet strongarm police tactics might have played a part. Two constables, Yardley and Moore, were criticized and disciplined for attacking a known scuttler one night after a rowdy party. The scuttler, John Ford, died four days after the attack, but the cause of death was attributed to pneumonia rather than the police beating. This case came to attention only because John Ford died, and it is widely accepted that unprovoked police beatings were routine in the area at this time.

As the twentieth century dawned, the influential *Manchester Guardian* editor, C.P. Scott, used the paper to complain that police were over-interpreting the Police Act of 1844 and using it to arrest lads just for going about their lawful business. To make matters worse, lads were only arrested for walking around in certain neighbourhoods, the poor ones, where scuttling had been a particular problem. No such punishment was used against youths wandering in the leafy suburbs. The echoes and comparisons to modern stop-and-search tactics are clear.

We will see elsewhere that rowdy behaviour is in some respects a routine part of childhood in general, and it is only a small minority who 'go too far' and veer into criminality. So, with the combined attractions of new football clubs, lads' clubs, the blossoming attractions of the American movies at the cinema, there were no more bored lads available to restock the gang membership as the older members settled down to married respectability. With more abundant work and more exciting leisure pursuits, the scuttlers simply grew out of their wild teenaged years and the attractions of gang membership, which had increased through the final decades of the nineteenth century, faded. The embarrassment of the country's failure to provide healthy men for the Boer War was also forgotten by the time the Great War began in 1914. The social context was changing, and scuttling came to be seen as unnatural, anti-social, and unpatriotic. There were bigger troubles on the horizon, and the gangs would unite to face an altogether more sinister foe.

This chapter in the history of Manchester and Salford youth lingers in the memory still. In the 1950s, when the now-elderly scuttlers were themselves terrified of the rise of the Teddy Boy, senior council leaders started to suggest flogging might deter this new trend. It is clear that flogging played no role in stamping out scuttling in the first place, although random police beatings might have had a slight impact, but society had moved on significantly by the decade of the Teddy Boy. Memories were vivid and stubborn. Andrew Davies unearthed a letter written as recently as 1995 in which Gladys Chorley, whose father keenly remembered the decades of the scuttlers, claimed that flogging stamped out the gang violence. These myths were handed down, but they were not true. Gang violence always returned.

Newcastle

The *Newcastle Daily Chronicle* of Saturday 8 November 1919 brings news of a gang of pickpockets routinely hassling passengers on the tramcars. They give the following sober warning: 'It is necessary once more to warn the general public against the gangs of pickpockets and bag-snatchers infesting the streets of Newcastle.' One sentence carries so much information. It is not the first time the paper has printed the warning, there is more than one gang, and they are roughly snatching bags as well as the more skilful and subtle art of emptying pockets unnoticed, and the paper hints that there are problems elsewhere, not just on the trams. The paper goes on to claim that there have been many such events in recent days to the extent that a warning is required. The general scam involved a small gang rushing onto the tramcar as it pulled into a stop. If the conductor happens to be on the upper deck, leaving the bottom deck clear, the gang gets to work. Otherwise, they wait for the next tram or try another stop.

On 8 June 1921 the same paper reported a different problem. Two men were sent to prison for a month with hard labour for stealing from a lock-up shop. Although they were described as professional men (one was a shoemaker, the other a tailor) it was claimed that they had travelled to the city in a group of ten men and based themselves at a lodging house for the purpose of wholesale burglary. In this one episode the two men got away with a clock, cartons of matches, chocolates and cigarettes. The police put forward a long history of similar crimes committed by the two, which can only have increased their punishment.

These are only the gang-related stories on these two days. The same page of the *Daily Chronicle* is festooned with all kinds of other crimes. After a miner had beaten his wife one evening, he was beaten up in turn by his wife's brothers. All five men found themselves in court. A former soldier was sent to prison for fraudulently claiming both 'out-of-work donation', a form of benefit, and disability allowance at the same time. A twenty year-old woman was charged with procuring a thirteen year-old girl for immoral purposes, a case that is reported in detail and caused significant concern among the authorities even though the eventual verdict was not guilty.

These are just a snapshot of a few stories in the news on the same day as the tramcar thieves were caught. Yet all three of them describe crimes that are likely to have been instigated from a situation of poverty. The case of the wounded soldier in particular feels like someone in difficult circumstances trying to make ends meet. Even the case of the professional burglars involved comparatively minor items, which were presumably chosen for their ease of resale and value-to-weight ratio.

On 30 May 1922, around a year later, the *Daily Chronicle* finds the burglars or 'shopbreakers' in the news once again. This time the defendants included a cartman, a labourer and a shoemaker who were sentenced to either three or six months in prison, having stolen a small amount of money plus 'large quantities' of cigarettes and chocolates with a total value of over £4. Again, the gang is rumoured to be ten strong and gradually being reduced through prison time. Sure enough, it is the same gang. One of the defendants is named as Cuthbert Armstrong, an eighteen-year-old shoemaker. After serving his time in 1919 he is on his way back to prison once again. This time the telling detail at the end of the report is this: 'They carried out their depredations in the most daring way, even removing bricks from walls in order to get into places.'

Our next story from the area shows that the horse racing gangs were active in Newcastle as they were elsewhere. The *Newcastle Chronicle and North Mail* of 30 November 1922 describes a Frederick Wensdale, twenty-one-years old, as a member of a gang who came to Leeds from Newcastle. Unfortunately, the story does not describe the precise nature of his crime, but he was officially charged with loitering with intent to commit a felony. Wensdale had previously been convicted in Doncaster, London and Blackpool and had only recently been discharged from Durham prison for a similar offence. He was sent straight back for three months with hard labour. The police claimed he was known to belong to a Newcastle gang engaged in a feud with a local Leeds gang and had brought some broken spectacles with him for the purpose of using the lenses either to defend himself or attack the rival gang.

The newspapers of 1920s' Newcastle have some of the same sorts of crimes you would find today. They do not often run to long analysis and are content to print a paragraph or two on each story, just giving the bare outline of what led to each trial. The exception is the case of a girl procured for immoral purposes, which generated almost a full column of discussion.

What we can see is that nobody could really get a balanced insight into the lives of the perpetrators from the newspapers. The reports are mainly noting down the charge, in technical language, the name, age and profession of the defendants, and then a comment or two on the police case against them. No indication of the context or background of the key characters. The most striking pattern is the severity of the sentences handed down for even comparatively minor offences. It is understandable that the authorities wanted to clamp down on repetitive professional burglary and gang-related feuds and pickpocketing. But six months of prison for stealing cigarettes and chocolates would be considered heavy-handed today, especially when the habitual horse-racing gang member got half that sentence.

June 1934 found the Newcastle gangs making the news in *The Scotsman*. The article uses some concerning language about 'alien thieves' and describes the gang as 'international' because some of the members, all Jewish, were not born in Britain. Nevertheless, the three who were caught seem to have been highly organized and professional. The specific incident described how they passed off pieces of glass as diamonds to a dealer in Newcastle. One member of the group in particular had an interesting history. Franz Ephraim Oberman, fifty-seven, was described as a Greek tailor from Paris. Originally from Uruguay, it was claimed that he 'had been known to the police of this country since 1930, and to the French, German and Austrian police since 1910'. Attempts to deport him previously had resulted in his escape. Oberman was the brother of another man in the dock on this occasion, known as Jacob Bercovitch but really Haim Oberman. Haim was known to Scotland Yard and had previously acted as an informant, once grassing on his brother. They had both served sentences in Pentonville prison before. All three of the glass con artists were sentenced to twenty-one months with hard labour.

Hull

In 1902 the *Hull Daily Mail* made passing reference to 'Hooliganism in Hull' in a general round-up article about a group called the Hull

Watch Committee at which the Chief Constable and various councillors discussed anti-social behaviour around Corporation Pier, today Victoria Pier near the famous Minerva pub. There is one reference to actual hooliganism on 23 July: 'Gangs of youths went prowling all over the town, and it was time a stop was put to it.' This line shows the limits of newspaper reporting. One councillor making one off-hand remark being quoted in the press. How many youths? How many days? Which areas of the town? This is the papers at their worst, vaguely stirring up cynical responses, but it does show that the idea of gangs, however loosely organized, were perceived to be at large by the turn of the century.

In 1925 George White, described as a 'fish bobber', found himself at Hull Police Court on an assault charge. A fish bobber was someone who worked on the docks where fishing trawlers were unloaded, and they would carry out a number of fairly specialized and labour-intensive tasks to unload the fish from the boats. Despite being employed, White was accused by the judge of belonging to a gang. The man assaulted was a steward of the New Savoy Club in Cleveland Street, then a private members' club, and his lawyer accused White of belonging to a gang. White denied it, and no evidence was offered, but it shows that there might have been some context to the affray that the *Hull Daily Mail* did not have room for. The episode is notable for the attitude of the magistrate, Robert Macdonald, who became well-known in Hull during these decades. He concluded with: 'We are not going to have any of this silly gang business in Hull.' The magistrate seems to suggest that the possibility of gangs operating in Hull is in the future rather than the present and is dismissively treated. Perhaps it shows the aloofness of the judiciary towards the working class youths seen elsewhere; perhaps there is an over confidence in the ability of the judiciary to prevent gangs, given that they only get involved after an offence is committed. But there is something in this attitude that is seen in the newspapers of the time: as soon as someone is associated with a gang, they stop being an individual. Putting the word gang or gangster into a headline almost guarantees it will be read, and whereas the press are trying to scare the public, the judiciary is for playing any problems down. In their own way, both sides indirectly encouraged the gangs through misunderstandings and disinterest in the lives of the individuals involved.

The magistrate's pleas were not heard. In June 1927, alongside a detailed report of that year's Epsom Derby, came news of another fracas in a private club after members had enjoyed a day at nearby Beverley racecourse. Arthur Gowthorpe was accused of assaulting a steward of the Sculcoates Club. Coincidentally, the magistrate was Robert Macdonald again who said at the end of this case: 'We have not heard much mention of gangs in Hull for a long, long time. Some cities are silly enough to go in for these so-called gangs. If we have any nonsense with gangs here every member will be dealt with as severely as I can possibly deal with him.'

Robert Macdonald was as good as his word. Gowthorpe was given two months' prison with hard labour, in stark contrast to George White in 1925 who got off with a fine. In this later Gowthorpe case, there was evidence of gang involvement. Gowthorpe got into the fight with an associate in the Sculcoates Club and, when police attended his house to arrest him, they found him barricaded inside with other men who were protecting him. No doubt Macdonald was frustrated but we have seen how little impact stern punishments would have on gang membership. The longer young men spent in prison, the more ingrained into the culture they became and the harder they found it to stay out of trouble.

By August 1928 one of the Hull gangs has a name: the Star Gang. There were some eye-catching details, and it seems likely there was a touch of humour in the reporting, though it is difficult to make out for the modern reader. The gang of nine boys were aged between seven and twelve and had been caught taking biscuits from the back of a wagon belonging to Associated Biscuits. The wagon had arrived to deliver biscuits to the London and North Eastern Railway. It seems unlikely that such a group would have been brought into court today, but this is an example of the court process itself being used as a deterrent for younger boys. They were all given a reprimand and let off, but no doubt the experience of being interviewed by police and placed in court before their parents would have been a sobering one. It is easy to see the logic behind this, and perhaps it worked in some cases, but it feels as if a better approach would have been to let the parents deal with such minor matters. Sometimes the experience of court did not deter future, more serious behaviour. The other notable aspect of this episode is that the magistrate noted the boys' membership of Sunday schools. The connection between idleness and criminality is explicitly acknowledged by the magistrate: 'He said that they were all to try and help each other to keep out of mischief, and the best thing they could do would be to join the Wolf Cubs or some similar organization, where they could still be banded in gangs, but would use their energy to a different and better end.' It was clearly understood that boys in particular naturally sought to form into like-minded groups, and that putting a sporting or scouting structure around those instincts was a positive step.

The following month, September 1928, found Robert Macdonald busy cleaning up gangs again, this time facing members of the 'Silver Hatchet Gang' in his courtroom. The newspaper hoped that the two months' prison with hard labour would be enough to warn other members to stop attacking members of the public. 'If it does not result in this end we sincerely hope that the still more severe punishment spoken of by the magistrate, when sentencing two of the "gang", will be meted out to all subsequent offenders.' In this editorial comment, we see how the newspapers tried to influence public opinion against the gangs. As soon as a crime was seen to be carried out by a 'gang', an abstract thing, rather than named individuals, all balance and sympathy was lost. A gang was not a person and a gang should be treated with the full penalty of the law, was the clear view of the newspaper's journalists, shared by the ever-vigilant Robert Macdonald. The article goes on to suggest that it was the arrival of cinema in Hull that led to gang violence, certain films glamourizing extreme violence, although the notorious *Scarface* was still a couple of years away. They acknowledge the tendency of young boys to band together naturally anyway and argue against giving them any additional excuse to cause trouble. More positive options for Hull's youth are suggested: the Scouts, Boys' Life Brigade and even the Territorial Army.

In December 1929 we meet Arthur Gowthorpe once again. He had been involved in the almost frivolous theft of a small amount of motor oil from a drum but it was his violent reactions afterwards that saw him before the court one more time. Gowthorpe had clearly not learned his lesson from the two months' hard labour he had received in 1927. Arthur Gowthorpe was still only 24 by this point and he was given another six months' hard labour, along with his accomplice, Henry Jennings Whittaker. Whittaker was already on probation at this time and the terms of his licence included staying away from Gowthorpe. This episode, perhaps more so than the earlier ones, shows one serious impact the gangs had on punishing the members. There is repeated reference to witnesses being too frightened to appear and, in the days with limited to no forensics, witnesses were essential in the absence of a confession. Simply by threatening the local population, even if the threats were never carried out, although they sometimes were of course, the gangs could ensure a certain protection for their members. The idea of the gang, so vague and abstract if pushed to explain it, held a tight grip on the minds of the law-abiding citizen. Gradually more frequent mention of the gangs in the newspapers would perpetuate an idea that the gangs were everywhere, and witnesses shrank from talking to the police as a result.

On the same page of the newspaper we are reminded again that prison sentences would not work to deter all offenders. A sixty-six-year-old man found himself in court for his sixtieth visit, making almost one court appearance a year for his whole life. William Patrick Ward, a seaman of no fixed address, had been caught stealing a jar of mint rock from a shop. His repeat offending ensured a stiff sentence of six months in prison for stealing the sweets. It seems unlikely that a further sentence would do anything positive for this habitual criminal, yet still the magistrate sent him to prison once again.

In July 1930 Robert Macdonald was busy again, but treading lightly this time. In a further example of how the gang myth can lead to side effects, a newspaper delivery man was in court for attacking a youth he believed to be a member of the gang. The attacker was Arthur Cracknell, and the police agreed that he had repeatedly been targeted and abused by gangs of youths. As so often happens, Cracknell had finally snapped and attacked young William Adamson, although Adamson himself was not believed to be part of the gang and was in the wrong place at the wrong time. Cracknell was given probation as he was generally law-abiding, but the episode shows how the tempers and tension caused by even localised gang abuse can drag down the general population.

In January 1932 a group of six youths was arrested for entering private residential and commercial properties for the purpose of stealing money from gas and electric meters. Perhaps they were not strictly a gang in the sense of a violent group, but they were collaborating together for commercial gain.

August 1937 brought another improbably-named Hull gang, the 'Dance Hall Gang', to public attention. Two teenagers faced the court accused of assault. Their victim was another youth of the same age and this time Macdonald dealt with the matter by binding them over, a form of probation, for six months. It was, in other words, a skirmish between boys of the same age. However, Robert Macdonald could not resist this tantalizing soundbite: 'The suggestion seems to be that it is a case of rival gangs, like Al Capone.' Anyone with even a passing acquaintance with the appalling, cynical crimes of Capone and his associates would have found the reference ridiculous, yet the paper repeated it with glee. In some ways, the paper was quite happy to exaggerate Hull's gang problem while at the same time professing a wish that it should be dealt with.

The suspicion that the *Hull Daily Mail* was using the flimsiest information to link young men, and some boys, to gang activity was strengthened in 1941. With a city at war, and many serious war stories on the same page, the paper reported that a gang member had been convicted on the charge of stealing woollen scarves from a railway warehouse. Although the police can only prosecute for offences where there is evidence, this sometimes leads to somewhat frivolous offences being charged rather than a youth's more serious antics. Nevertheless, the twenty-one-year-old man was accused of leading many boys astray while they were on probation and of being the ring leader of a gang. The magistrate, the busy Robert Macdonald, threatened to send him to borstal.

In 1935 there was a Broadway play called *Dead End*, directed by Sidney Kingsley. It was turned into a film and was played in Hull in 1938, and at many UK cinemas nationwide. It was so successful that it became a series of films, making stars of its actors, who became known as the 'Dead End Kids'. Then, in November 1940, a group of youths was arrested who claimed to be equipping themselves to fight a gang they called the Dead End Kids. The Dead End Kids gang became so notorious that the *Hull Daily Mail* started a campaign to get the members locked up.

The first newspaper reference to the Dead End Kids occurred on 25 November 1940 and it was an indirect reference. A group of young men had been arrested in Silver Street after a drinking session at the Blue Bell pub in Hull's ancient marketplace, known today as Ye Olde Blue Bell. Their improbable crime was the theft of one glass tumbler and one bar stool. The four arrested were Ronald Dry, eighteen, Harry Smith, nineteen, Reginald Vollans, twenty, and Allan Fellow, nineteen. Their comparatively young age is a hallmark of most of the gangs we have encountered on this journey. They were tooling up for a fight, intending to break the legs off the stool to use them as batons. But this was a defensive move, claimed the lads. They were afraid of an organized gang they referred to as the Dead End Kids and needed to arm themselves should they be attacked. The eldest defendant, Reginald Vollans, spoke for the group. He claimed the Dead End Kids were around twenty-five lads in strength and they always stalked around in large groups, so they were impossible to defend against without weapons. The gang were also claimed to use knuckledusters, further enhancing their powers. These young lads, they claimed, were in mortal fear. Whatever the story behind this short article from the *Hull Daily Mail*, it gives us a date at which the Dead End Kids were fully organized and striking fear into the residents. It is possible that the four in the dock were associates of the Dead End Kids, or perhaps they belonged to a rival gang and were not the blameless innocents they claimed to be. At any rate, for the Dead End Kids to have grown to a membership of twenty-five by the end of 1940 suggests they had been in operation for many months by then, and possibly over a year.

In February 1941, just a few months after they were first mentioned by the paper, two of the Dead End Kids appear in another article. Although they were only fifteen and sixteen, they were already banned from various dance halls and billiards rooms for violence at this point, again adding weight to the assumption that the gang had been in operation for many months at least. This time the offence was a smash-and-grab raid on a jewellers in Anlaby Road called Branton's. Items to the value of £72 were stolen. The youths smashed the window on the night of 14 January, making a hole just big enough for an arm to fit through. The pair sold six stolen rings to a man they did not know in a cinema, and through these rings the defendants were eventually traced. One youth made the unlikely claim that he had thrown many rings into the River Hull, but in any event, only £16 worth of jewellery was recovered. The boys were so young that their fathers were summoned to court and ordered to keep closer tabs on their sons. The younger boy paid a small fine and was placed on probation, and the older boy was remanded into custody for one week. In a related case in the same edition of the newspaper, a seventeen-year-old was charged at Hull Police Court with receiving three of the rings knowing them to be stolen. This boy was fined but given a strict warning that he would be placed in borstal for three years if he appeared before the court again.

By 21 April 1941 things were getting out of hand. An article on that date claimed that the gang was finally to be 'broken up' for good. After a fracas involving fifteen of the Dead End Kids in the entrance of a dance hall, two of the boys were finally sent to prison. Other members of the gang were believed to be present in the court for the purpose of intimidating witnesses. In fact, the two were sent to prison for a very short time, one for two months and the other for only two weeks, casting doubt on the newspaper's claim that the gang was being broken up. The police claimed to have six officers trying to keep control of the gang of around twenty youths, which sounds like a high number, but the frustration of the police and the courts at repeatedly seeing the same youths, all under the age of twenty-three, is clear.

Scepticism would not have been misplaced in 1941 that the Dead End Kids were on the way out. They appear again as late as 1944, and possibly still later than that. On 25 November 1944, with the war fading out, two of the gang stole a US Army jeep and drove it recklessly around town for two hours with the Military Police in hot pursuit. The older of the two, although only twenty, Gordon Dickenson, was an airman himself. He was fined for taking the vehicle without consent and for driving without a licence or insurance. The jeep was stolen outside the swimming baths on Beverley Road and driven along Walton Street and Anlaby Road into the centre of Hull. The Military Police officer, who was following in another jeep, managed to crash into the stolen vehicle, in which chaos one of the youths jumped out and ran off. Although the youth who escaped, Martin Jackson, was only seventeen, he was described as the leader of the Dead End Kids. This explains why he got more than just a fine. He was sent to prison for six weeks with hard labour.

A feature article in the *Hull Daily Mail* of August 1948 relates the story of a local man intent on removing Hull's gangs from the streets by organizing clubs. This is a more constructive approach than having a magistrate issue quiet warnings, mainly unheeded, to boys who had already gone out of control and is in line with similar organizations elsewhere in Britain. The paper suggests that the war years were a particular problem for young boys because their fathers were away fighting the war and their mothers had taken up work in their absence, leaving them without close role models for much of the day. The Chief Constable of Hull Police, Mr T. Wells, created the Hull City Police Boys'

Clubs in 1943 to try and set an example for the boys. This is an unusual approach from the police themselves to set the local boys straight, rather than leaving it to the Scouts or grassroots football clubs. Just five years later, in 1948, there were 650 boys enrolled, helped by sixty volunteers, all of them police officers or their wives, relatives and close friends. It was a shrewd move because it helped young boys see that the police staff were also human, and it would also presumably give the police early warning if some boys misbehaved.

Sheffield

Sheffield works well as a comparison to Hull and Birmingham, being somewhere in the middle in terms of population size in 1920. Sheffield had around 600,000 inhabitants, Hull half that at under 300,000 and Birmingham nudging up towards one million.

Just like other papers of the time, the *Sheffield Daily Independent* tried to play down the local gang nuisance at the same time as confirming that a problem did exist. 'Birmingham and Leeds have been mentioned frequently, but Sheffield is not free from the nuisance.' The paper admitted that Sheffield gangs did pester racegoers but suggested that they were non-violent, limiting themselves to pickpocketing and short con tricks such as the three-card trick or finding the lady. The gang's activities away from the racecourse were more sinister, threatening pub landlords with physical violence if they refused to pay arbitrary 'tolls' as protection money. The newspaper explains the general process used by the gang: 'Usually, a gang enters the house and drinks are ordered. When payment is requested the licensee (landlord) is told that "It is all right" and shortly afterwards there is a request to the landlord to lend "a fiver" to the gang. The alternative is the smashing of glasses and windows, and assaults.' The more nervous landlords are singled out and the more courageous ones avoided. This interesting commentary article is from 1921 and claims there are exactly four gangs operating in the city. Unfortunately, no gang names are given. This number is unlikely to be correct because we know from elsewhere how loosely organized so many other gangs were. The article ends by suggesting that the gangs do use violence on the racecourse, in contradiction of its more downplayed introduction.

By 1922 the *Sheffield Independent* was treading a less controversial line, at least locally, by sending a reporter down to London to report on the notorious Sabinis and other gangs around the city. Perhaps Sheffield residents felt more secure knowing that the danger was almost two hundred miles away. One important contribution in that year's August silly season was to note that the racecourse gangs were really much more generalized crime gangs. "'There is scarcely a big robbery in London," said a police officer, in the course of conversation, "that cannot be traced to these so-called racing gangs. In reality they are crime gangs.'" In other words, they were purely and simply violent organized crime gangs who were active in a number of spheres, of which the racecourse was just the most publicly visible example.

On 6 May 1925, nine men, members of racing gangs, were in court in Sheffield charged with the murder of a sixty-year-old Sheffield resident, William Francis Plommer, who had been attacked by a gang at Norfolk Bridge. The victim had been stabbed with a putty knife, of all things, and attacked with a blunt instrument believed to be a poker. *The Aberdeen Press and Journal* suggests that 'Plommer met his death during an affray between two of the notorious gangs which have for some years been a source of trouble to the Sheffield police'. The nine accused ranged in age from the early twenties to forty and the case was adjourned for further preparation. That the case was reported as far away as Aberdeen shows that there was nationwide interest in gang activities. Two of the men were hanged for the murder in September of 1925 at Leeds. Wilfrid Fowler was hanged by Albert Pierrepoint, the notorious executioner of his time, and, a day later, his brother Lawrence was hanged. In a last desperate act, Wilfrid had sworn a statement that Lawrence had no role in the murder but it was too late to save him and perhaps the evidence against him was too strong. However their victim came to be killed, whether by calculation or accident, it shows that gang members could expect to be executed for killing, even if the killing was inadvertent and their victims were also members of gangs. This explains why they took trouble to avoid such extreme incidents, and this is a comparatively rare event even for the 1920s.

Leeds

The first mention of gangs in Leeds of the twentieth century that caught my eye came on 20 May 1902. An article in the *Yorkshire Post* documented a gang of twenty-five youths in the Marsh Lane district who were organized into a gang and carried out violent robberies in the area, targeting 'drunken men' which looks like a veiled reference to vagrants. However, only two men appeared in the dock and received sentences of two and three months. The response of the courts is striking in the case of the defendant George Tyreman. The Leeds Stipendiary Magistrate, Mr Atkinson, believed that Tyreman came from a 'respectable' family and had fallen in with the wrong crowd. Although the men were sent to prison in an attempt to break their association, Atkinson is not optimistic but he is unusually supportive: 'It was understood that assistance would be given to Tyreman to get away if he still desires it after coming out of prison.'

At the end of January 1912 the *Yorkshire Evening Post* was moved to describe in detail the activities of Leeds card sharps because so many victims had been fleeced that month, typically on a train where the unsuspecting punter became a captive audience with time to kill. As seen elsewhere, the card trick gangs concentrated on those who might be short of confidence, this time, a businessman recently returned from Canada and a German salesman. Each lost around £40 trying to 'find the lady' by chance out of a choice of three cards. The gang of four or five men would enter a quiet railway compartment in which a lone male would be seated. They would pretend not to know each other and fall in with a game of guessing for small wagers. The men would always win, which tended to make their 'mug' think that he had a chance of making some quick money. Of course, as soon as the mug entered the game, the Queen card would not be seen again. There was no chance of him winning any money at all, and if he became irritated or angry the gang would melt away and leave the train at the next station. The paper incredulously notes that this happens 'in broad daylight' before adding the kicker: 'before dinner!'

Because gambling was illegal, and due to the shame of being conned, it was highly unusual for a victim to report the matter to police. Added to that the mobile nature of the crime made it hard to track down suspects, and even to decide which police force should investigate the crime. The gang knew just how to escape arrest, more often than not.

In December 1926 the *Berks and Oxon Advertiser*, without a local gang story but keen to get in on the action, reported an incident from Leeds. A former bookmaker, Joseph Burns, aged forty-three, was given a huge six years' penal servitude for the relatively minor charge of two counts of demanding money with menaces. It was Detective Sergeant Noble who filled in the character of Burns, accusing him of living from the proceeds of his threats and blackmail as a member of a racing gang. His victims were usually too frightened to report his attacks. This was not just the opinion of one police officer, either. Burns had previously served five years for manslaughter, after which sentence he was returned to prison for causing grievous bodily harm. Given Burns' age and history, it seems unlikely that further prison time would reform his behaviour, but the judge felt he had to be kept off the streets. He described Burns as a 'dangerous man who must be sent where he could not terrorise the public, as the first step, which must be a vigorous one, to break up these gangs'. As was common for men with children, Burns asked not to be sent away due to the harm it would cause his young family. We know that many such men found it difficult to empathize with their future selves and think ahead to how their families might suffer in their absence. "I always think," said the judge, "that this world would be a better place if men who intend to commit these crimes would think of their wives and little ones before they acted.'"

In January 1935 the *Nottingham Evening Post* was thrilled to report problems in Leeds with unusually young children involved in thieving for gangs. Reports had been published describing the problem when children younger than teenagers were exploited to steal from warehouses and other commercial premises. The children were said to be working for gaming clubs, of which twenty-three were closed down the previous year. During that year the Leeds Juvenile Court had seen 138 boys and 11 girls for various theft offences, showing how disproportionately boys found themselves drawn into such activities. However, the report noted particularly that 'In one case a gang consisted entirely of girls aged eight to 12'.

Later that year, in September, the *Hull Daily Mail* pitched in on the issues in Leeds, a much larger city with proportionately more problems. The naive journalists loudly proclaimed that a Leeds gang had been 'broken up' yet the leader, William Stockhill, received only a twelve-month sentence and his three sidekicks got six months or less. Their younger associates had already been dispersed to borstals. The notion that a few months in prison would be enough to change their behaviour and forever end the existence of the gang was shown elsewhere to be optimistic. Still, it took them out of action for several months. One of the notable facts about this case is that the men all had skilled jobs and were not idling around the city.

In the summer of 1936, Shipley, a town just north of Bradford near Leeds, decided to organize its own boys' club. Ideas first carried out in the big cities were moving to the smaller towns. Shipley Urban Council and the Yorkshire Association of Boys' Clubs were involved, as was the Shipley Rotary Club. The committee discussed how boys' clubs were oversubscribed as soon as they began, showing high demand, yet only one in seven and sometimes one in twelve boys had a suitable club in their area. The president of Shipley Rotary was clear in his mind, said the *Shipley Times & Express*, that 'A boy leaving school and going into industry comes up against a set of circumstances he has never met before. He thinks he has put school behind him and has suddenly become a man, and unless something is done for him he may become the wrong type of man.'

The Middleton Estate in Leeds hit the news in October 1937 after six teenaged boys appeared on charges including theft. All but one of the boys had appeared in court before. The magistrate was worried that if they were all sent to the local remand home then they would stay together as a unit and continue to conspire with each other. Therefore he took the step of sending them to Armley Gaol for a week while they could be arranged places in 'approved schools'. The magistrate blamed the parents: 'Apparently there is not one of you who really tries to exercise the care which ought to be taken. Middleton is becoming one of the worst areas of Leeds. There is a whole series of boys down there who get the idea that everything is fair game. They plunder and loot and do anything they like.'

All kinds of problems with breaking and entering, vandalism, robbery and assault were a persistent problem on the Middleton Estate throughout the winter of 1937–8. However, January 1938 brought some good news. Credit for the turnaround was given to the parents of local children who had agreed to keep closer control of their offspring, and various Christmas parties had been arranged to keep them off the streets. This small episode showed just how quickly trouble could be averted with co-operation from various local organizations and parents, and would have been boosted by the burgeoning numbers of local boys' clubs.

Leeds also had its share of problems with juveniles after the war started. The usual cause is attributed to absent fathers away fighting while their mothers were involved in war-related jobs near home. In April 1940 the *Yorkshire Evening Post* set out some statistics. In the previous day alone, over sixty boys had faced various charges in the juvenile court. The problem, according to the chairman of the Bench, Dr Walter Parsons, had been getting steadily worse during the winter of 1939–40, which does line up well with the outbreak of war. In the year to April, the same court had seen 467 cases compared to 290 for the same period the previous year, before war broke out. Dr Parsons muses on the idea of fining parents who cannot bring their children into line. The article attributes the main cause of the upsurge in delinquency to be the closure of schools. Some boys had not seen a classroom for nine months. Just as in the recent pandemic, the authorities had 'paid too much attention on the physical dangers of war among the civil population, and not sufficient to the moral dangers'. Dr Parsons was surely ahead of his time when he observed that 'I am not so sure that the moral danger is not greater than the physical danger' and that 'there was a lack of foresight and vision in the long closure of schools'.

One of the most desperate cons I found anywhere was the case of forty-year-old Thomas Grundy in April 1946. He had been caught 'exchanging rags for toys' with a 'child under 14'. He was caught near a school but did not appear in person in court and was fined £3 or a month in prison if he did not pay. The police said Grundy was not acting alone and was a known member of an unnamed Leeds gang. The crime sounds slightly ridiculous but this was claimed to be a lucrative scheme and was a cynical exploitation of school children. It is not known if the gang were only involved in these small-time cons or whether they were part of the violent groups, but Grundy is at the top end of the age range for violent gang membership.

By August 1948 Leeds was struggling with a different problem. The *Yorkshire Evening Post* reported that gangs had been robbing freight trains to the extent of £2.5 million per year which forced the railway authorities to change strategy. Some of the high value goods were the expected wines and spirits, but in a sign of the troubles after the Second World War, clothes and shoes also attracted the attention of thieves. In prior years, as rail freight increased, it might have been assumed that goods travelling at high speed on trains were safe from interception by criminal gangs. However, it did not take the gangs long to find the weak spot: whenever a train was stationary in remote sidings they could quite easily gain access to high value goods. It was time for a new idea and perhaps this was the start of modern approaches which include armoured vans for cash deliveries, for example. Working together, the railway authorities, their customer manufacturers who transported goods by rail, and the police, came up with the idea of using 'secret' railway sidings to shunt and transfer goods, which would be unknown to gang members, at least for a time. In addition, they used locked and guarded railway carriages, and when the goods were transferred to the road for the final leg of their journey, the lorries were also locked. There was no stage of the journey when the valuable goods were not locked up, and for the weak links in the process police guards were also present. Goods from all over the north of England, including Carlisle, Barrow, Heysham and Huddersfield, were directed to the secret Leeds siding for onward travel to the end customers in the south. It would have increased the transport costs significantly, which shows how big a problem it had become for such a scheme to be less expensive than the theft of the goods.

The *Evening Telegraph* of 23 October 1942 relates a Leeds burglary in unusual detail. The five men and one woman who were charged in connection with the robbery were notable by their varied addresses. A man from Maidenhead, Berkshire, one from Plymouth and one from the Great Yarmouth town of Gorleston-on-Sea. Four of the men were current or former members of the British Army, which gives a clue as to how they knew each other. Indeed, two of them wore their uniforms to the burglary itself. All the men were charged with 'robbery with violence' and the woman, Mrs Katherine Woods, was charged with conspiracy to commit robbery. Her husband was not involved in the crime. This was a big crime: £926 in case was stolen and around £4,000 in jewellery.

Chapter 6

Gangs of Scotland and Ireland

As we have seen elsewhere, every major city has considered itself to have a serious gang problem at one time or another. Most of them awake on a certain morning to find themselves living in the 'worst city in Europe' for gangs, according to their local newspaper. Most likely, other European cities made the same observations as Britain. In this chapter we look at Scotland and Ireland.

Glasgow

It was the summer of 1930 when, according to Andrew Davies in his excellent *City of Gangs: Glasgow and the Rise of the British Gangster*, Glasgow's *Evening Citizen* realised that something had to change. Apparently everyone in the rest of the world now considered Glasgow to be the most violent city on earth, a true 'city of gangs'. There were dozens of them, with perhaps 7,000 active members, causing havoc among the law-abiding Glaswegians.

The gangs became perceived as a problem when they started to stray outside their own patches of the city. When the young lads of Cowcaddens, a slum on the northern edge of Glasgow, fought each other, nobody seemed to mind. It was when their violence began to spread further afield and involve attacks on the general public that the police, the courts and the newspapers started to investigate.

The most striking aspect of the gangs as they were when the twentieth century began is the young age of their members. They really were teenagers, with peak gang membership, and peak violence, occurring from the age of fifteen upwards. At a time when schooling was only compulsory until the age of ten, and many lads were in full-time employment before they reached thirteen, it is clear that the concept of teenagers and young adults then was very different to now. They were not only school-leavers doing fulltime adult work, which could be very dangerous, perhaps in the factories or coal mines, but they were allowed to drink alcohol and were adults in every social and legal sense. They were legally accountable for their actions in the eyes of the police and the courts.

1906 seems to have been a pivotal year for Glasgow's gangs: it was the year they really broke into the public conscience. At that time the *Glasgow Herald* claimed there were a dozen serious gangs in the city, not just groups of kids standing on street corners, and the largest of those dozen had hundreds of members. The gangs were normally divided on sectarian lines, with the rare exception being the San Toy, from Calton, which mixed Catholics and Protestants.

As in Dublin and Belfast, there were moments when crime and sectarian violence overlapped. Along with the violence came the protection rackets: the disingenuous extending of 'protection' services to those people and businesses who were prepared to stump up cash. It was the very same people offering the protection who would vandalize, steal, or torture to demonstrate just how necessary and valuable their protection could be.

Glasgow is perhaps even more famous than Dublin for its tenements. These grand old houses, invariably with their best days behind them, found themselves used as mass accommodation for the poorest citizens. This not only brought health problems but the sheer density of population caused nerves to fray. Too much time, not enough money, and no privacy, often boiled over into fights and worse. This density combined with a poor employment situation meant that Glasgow's gang troubles were likely to be worse than those in England, even in London.

And just as Liverpool had an edge of sectarian conflict between Protestant and Catholic gangs, it was worse in Glasgow. Even today, football crowds have that undertone of sectarianism: supporting either Celtic or Rangers is never a simple footballing choice.

Guns were hardly ever used, because even hardened gang members did not want to risk the death penalty. On one rare occasion, again in 1906, when a gang member, John McAndrew, was shot and killed, and the perpetrator was held before a court, he was acquitted. The shooter, Joseph Ventura, had been terrified of gang activity in and around his ice cream parlour, and had brought out his rifle in self-defence. The jury agreed.

Just as in England, the gangs used horse racing as a platform to make money. Initially they were careful and blackmailed only the English bookmakers at Scottish racecourses. But the Scottish gangs wanted to target the same bookmakers, and violence flared up. By the end of that troubled year, 1906, gang violence waned again. Or, at least, it vanished from the front pages of the newspapers. After the police brought forward dubious statistics 'proving' that gang violence was not such a problem after all, the press and general public lost interest. That is not the same thing as the violence itself subsiding but, from this remove over a century later, it is interesting to consider that, when newspapers are your main source of on-the-spot news coverage, if events cease to be written about evidence of them fizzles out. Like the tree falling in the empty forest, it is difficult to know with certainty whether the gang violence did wane after 1906 or whether the public just lost interest. Most likely it was a bit of both. Then, as now, people debated with some vigour whether the media just reflected local concerns or whether the journalists had a hand in stirring up trouble.

It was a decade before Glasgow's gangs took hold of the public imagination once again. With the Great War in full swing, the ranks of the police were depleted and the nighttime streets fell dark. Perfect conditions for the Glasgow youths, and others elsewhere in Britain, to revive their love of the gang spirit. Those involved were either too young to fight in the war, or they were exempt from conscription because they worked in factories making war equipment. Not surprisingly, the press was quick to proclaim that this new generation of gang members were even more violent than their forebears. With horse racing largely stopped on the British mainland for the duration of the war, the new gangs turned their attention to the comfortable patrons of the dance halls. A cap would be handed around for cash and valuables to be given up in exchange for protection from violence. Ironically, one of the excuses put forward by the police for losing control of the city, in addition to their depleted numbers, was the enforcement of new legislation that forced them to round up deserters rather than focus on what the public and the press considered to be real criminals. The British national papers seized their opportunity to embarrass Scotland, and a new panic began.

If in 1906 the police understated the threat from gangs, there is no doubt that the 1916 press overstated the case. Just as in Manchester, the weak discipline at school, coupled with weak and absent parental role models, were blamed for the perceived rise in violence. As in Manchester, the remedy was more forceful policing and more draconian court sentences. But surely if the cause truly was as simple as blaming schools and parents, then the solution should have been found there. It seems bizarre from this safe distance to think that a deficiency in one part of a young lad's life can be corrected by draconian punishment coming from another direction altogether, and from strangers too. Nevertheless, and notwithstanding their depleted numbers, the police did mount a crackdown. Even noisy behaviour in public could attract the attention of the police after the panic took hold in the summer of 1916.

As elsewhere in Britain, the violence worsened when the war ended. A surplus of young men, hardened by battle and with new fighting skills, came home to a shortage of jobs. And this is the period when the hooligans and gang lads began to be labelled as *gangsters*. It was an American word, and one that I try to avoid where possible in this book. It is dehumanizing and so loaded with negative connotation as to make the problems in reporting this period worse. The evidence clearly shows that the youths were not inherently violent. It took a particular combination of boredom, energy, poverty and weak role models, or other societal conditions, to generate the conditions for a flare-up in gang violence. No doubt, there were some career criminals mixed in with the innocent teenagers, and the older boys, the young men in their twenties, must also take some of the blame for recruiting and perpetuating gang membership among their younger neighbours and siblings. But the terminology around the gangster makes the problem even worse, and simplifies the problem, even blames the gang activities on the younger boys, those who would come to be seen as victims.

The use of the word gangster is misleading when you try to compare the activities of the British gangs against their American counterparts. The Glasgow newspapers brought word of the most notorious Chicago gangsters, Jack Diamond and Al Capone, during the American prohibition era when alcohol was not allowed to be sold in bars. But in these stories, which carried more than a hint of thrilling entertainment, guns and murder appeared routine. Bearing in mind that Glasgow at this time worried that it had the worst gang violence in Europe, death was rare and virtually always inadvertent. Guns were hardly ever seen on the streets and, if they were, they were shown as a deterrent and not fired.

Just as the 1906 panic subsided within a few months, so did the 1916 gang panic. The workers were uniting together in unions. Disputes were threatening the efficiency of the factories making munitions and ships for the war effort. After the war ended the disputes became more bitter. A general strike in January 1919 led to a stand-off between the workers and the police which bore the hallmarks of a riot. Projectiles were thrown at the police, who used baton charges in response. Thousands of troops, including tanks and machine guns, were stationed in the city the following day. If the move was intended to calm nerves, it can easily be imagined that it achieved the opposite effect. Even the national press waded into the delicate situation, proclaiming that the army had occupied Glasgow. Nobody worried about the teenagers in the gangs now. This pendulum swing between fear of gang violence and other matters, whether it be war, industrial unrest, or the perceived collapse of social patterns, continued. It feels as though the public only worried about the gangs when the press had nothing else to write about.

Thus without money, the euphoria of surviving the Great War soon dissipated. Matters turned to survival for some, which was felt more keenly when the middle classes were cavorting in new dance halls and experimenting with extra leisure time in other ways. How fair was this new society, when some children fought over stale food in puddles and dilapidated houses while other children copied American fashion from the cinemas and quaffed milkshakes while dancing the night away in garishly illuminated ballrooms? Trouble was inevitable.

Perhaps this time, in 1918 and beyond, it was different. Authorities across Britain, including the press, worried about the effects of war on young minds. Even those who had not fought had experienced the effects of war: the loss of family members, extreme mental torment in those returning home, the loss of work which led to recession, which led to poverty and more crime. And just as people were hoping to turn their back on conflict, problems between Catholics and Protestants in Ireland spread to Glasgow with its own sectarian tensions. Trouble erupted again when a police officer was shot and killed in an attempt to free Frank Carty, an IRA commander, who was being carried in a police van to Duke Street prison in the city. However, despite such eye-catching episodes, the feared uprising never happened. Although it seems logical to worry about young men with time on their hands returning from war with newly acquired violent skills, the majority had seen more than enough to last a lifetime and simply wanted peace.

It was not until the early 1920s that the press began to worry about lesser, though still significant, levels of violence. Just like Birmingham's Peaky Blinders, the Glasgow gangs also took up the razor and made it a hallmark of their trade. The razor and other blades still strike fear into the hearts of law-abiding citizens. They draw comparison with modern-day acid attacks in the sense that the cynical purpose of such attacks is to scar, not to kill. The gangs knew that murder was too risky in a time of capital punishment, but they also found that their targets were more worried about permanent maiming or scarring than a quick death. The fear of a slashing to the face was powerful in itself, even if no attack took place.

As if to prove that capital punishment was no deterrent, the hanging of John Keen for the racist murder of Noor Mohammed had no discernible impact on gang violence, which again flared up along sectarian lines during the Orange Order parade in July 1925. But in 1926 the gangs were eclipsed once again by industrial unrest. Would the pendulum ever stop? And in such circumstances, how could anyone claim to understand all the complex causes of gang violence?

One striking aspect of the reporting of violence is how quickly the press and public turn to the police for answers, never seeming to analyze their own ambivalence until a single eye-catching event forces some acknowledgement that all is not well. The very same parents who turn a blind eye to the youthful exuberance of their own children blame the police rather than their neighbours when exuberance turns to more serious criminality. Once this pattern is noticed, it can be seen to repeat around Britain and feels like an ingrained trait of human behaviour: every problem is someone else's responsibility to solve.

Predictably, by 1927 the press was again putting forward the idea that flogging these razor-slashing hooligans would solve the problem. Again, the press acknowledges that the youths were themselves victims of the appalling poverty and attendant boredom in the slums of Glasgow. Why is it that, instead of looking to solve the perennial problem of poverty, which the newspapers themselves claimed to be the cause of the gang violence, were they instead suggesting corporal punishment and long prison sentences? Because the latter can be achieved with the stroke of a pen, whereas poverty would take decades of meticulous investment and nurturing. It is unlikely that the public and the authorities really believed the lash or whip would solve the problems caused by poor living conditions and unemployment, but there was pressure to find quick answers. If they acknowledged, as they did, that there was something romantic and enticing about the danger of gang membership, why could they not see that increasing the penalties might inadvertently increase the sense of adventure in the lifestyle?

Billy Fullerton: a real gang leader in 1932

Billy Fullerton led the infamous Billy Boys gang. Fullerton was released from prison in 1932 after serving a sentence for assaulting the police. Around six hundred local residents had risked reprisal to sign a petition which, although somewhat coded in its phrasing, demanded protection from Billy's violent gang. Fullerton was warned not to return to gang violence on his release from prison, or risk a much longer stretch in a remote, notorious prison up at Peterhead, with the added deterrent of penal servitude. Perhaps surprisingly, Fullerton did renounce his membership of the eponymous Billy Boys gang, and his role as King Billy. Surprisingly for the time, he then sold his story to the press. He used the article to renounce violence and requested he be left to a quiet life with his wife and children.

Fullerton's early life bears closer inspection because of the clues it gives to the way individuals found themselves drawn to violence and crime. Until he was nineteen, there is no evidence that Fullerton was set for a life as a gang leader. He left school at fourteen, which was routine at the time, and completed his apprenticeship as a boilermaker. But his nineteenth year coincided with the difficult economic situation of 1925. His employer let him go when he qualified for adult wages, on the cynical excuse that a younger lad would be cheaper to hire and be almost as productive. This was a clear loophole in the labour laws, and one that advantaged the employers at the expense of the local lads trying to make a living. But Fullerton was not deterred. Showing his determination to succeed, he decided to try his luck in Canada. He set off as a ship's fireman and all went well until the work ran out and he was laid off again, this time in Canada. Yet again, Fullerton demonstrated his resourcefulness. He managed to find a ship to take him back to Scotland where he moved in with his parents and worked in the local cinema. Even though this must have felt like a drop in responsibility for a qualified boilermaker, Fullerton took it in his stride.

Fullerton only slips into a gang, the suitably-named Billy Boys, after a violent altercation stemming from his work in the cinema. The gang was already established before they approached him to become their leader. After he helped eject a group of fighting youths from the cinema, they caught up with him near his home and attacked him with weapons including a hammer. Enraged beyond logic, Fullerton took on the gang members with his bare hands. When news of his bravery reached the Billy Boys, they suggested he join them so that they could offer him protection from the other gang. Although the precise details of this conversion changed over the years, there seems little doubt that Fullerton found himself sucked into the gang life inadvertently. His life until that point shows significant resourcefulness against a backdrop of economic hardship. He had even travelled across the Atlantic and back again to find legitimate employment.

This is a pattern we have seen many times across the whole of Britain: that the precise causes of gang violence are complex, but a backdrop of economic stagnation and poverty leads to a climate in which street violence becomes so common that it is noticed by the general public. The spiral unfolds, and even law-abiding citizens who are determined to live by the rules get dragged into the malign influence of the gangs.

Fullerton married Rose Ann Farmer in October 1926, when she was eighteen and he was twenty. Four days later, the Billy Boys leader found himself on trial on an assault charge. He was sentenced to three months with hard labour and he began to view incarceration differently now that he was married. He did make attempts to leave the gang after his release, but the Boys respected him and applied pressure on him to return as their leader. Billy did return and restored the fortunes of the gang. He was good at it and enjoyed organizing. He seems to have had a rare mix of skills in fighting, leadership and organization. It is clear that if he had been dealt another hand in his teenage years, he would have been a successful boilermaker and manager. At this point, during yet another prison sentence, Billy met a prison visitor involved in the early Boy Scout movement, Major Malcolm Speir. Speir spent a lot of time with Fullerton and even found him a job after his release. Fullerton took up boxing as an outlet for his energies and seemed to have made a fresh start. But he was a target for members of other gangs, and he was frequently attacked, even when carrying his young child. He did manage to hold down the new job but violence was never far away and it was not until 1932 that he finally renounced gang membership and violence. He took to the pages of the *Weekly News* for an interview which served as an advertisement to the gang population of Glasgow: Billy Fullerton had permanently retired and wanted to be left in peace to look after his young family.

Fullerton's association with Major Speir became known publicly only in 1955. It became known in 1931 that Speir had sometimes administered corporal punishment as part of his prison visitor role, and that this was known to the police. Speir saw nothing wrong with his actions at the time, although they were illegal, and he boasted to a journalist that he had given a Billy Boys leader a thrashing. Perhaps there were rumours, but it was not until 1955 that Fullerton admitted Speir had thrashed him with the knowledge of his father, who was present in an adjoining room.

It took Fullerton years to finally leave the gang life behind him and he was repeatedly attacked and provoked by others in an attempt to keep him locked into the gang scene. It was impossible to obtain a job and keep one if you were a known gang member, so the whole ecosystem sustained itself. Billy stood out as a fighter and leader, and so perhaps greater efforts were made to keep him in the gang, but it is easy to see how a less determined man, perhaps one without a wife and young children, would not have the strength of character to walk away from such a life. Then, as now, rumour could make or break a reputation and Billy's actions had been repeatedly recorded in the press and in the prison records. He was a marked man and it took an extraordinary will to go straight. By July 1933 his transformation was complete: he reformed the Billy Boys as a legitimate boys' club with premises and a piano, a billiard table and a boxing ring. He even found himself courted by local dignitaries and was elected the club's first president. The transformation of these new premises had been helped by unemployed skilled tradesmen from the local area. Perhaps this story more than any other across Glasgow, from any decade, shows how complex the gang problem was, and also how fear and physical punishment could not in the end bring a stop to it. It just needed people to whom the gang members looked up, which would not include the police or the courts, to show them a different way of life.

Although the 1950s is seen as the decade when American culture really took its grip on Britain, in fact it started after the Great War. For all the colour of the 1950s, the 1920s was the *noir* period. Hollywood still predominantly peddled black-and-white films, and film buffs might disagree on exactly which was the first 'talkie' but it was not until the end of the 1920s. So the 1920s' teenager had less in the way of technological advancement than the 1950s' kids, but the influence of America was not dimmed by that. Worse still for the forces of law and order, Hollywood decided to push high profile gangster movies such as *Scarface* in 1932. How on earth were the authorities to keep a lid on these tensions caused by religion, poverty, and now stoked high by Hollywood entertainment?

Gang members were unmistakable. Just as the Peaky Blinders were known for their sharp dressing and stylized caps on the head, the Glasgow gang member dressed just as finely. His hat was known as a 'bunnet' but the effect was the same: people would cross the road to avoid running into these youths. Spurred on by heroes such as Al Capone, or at least a Hollywood version of him, the gangs even aped American slang on the streets of Glasgow. Andrew Davies explains that, although Glasgow was sometimes known as 'Scottish Chicago', hardly anyone was ever killed there, compared to around 500 gang-related murders in the American Chicago.

No Mean City: A Novel?

Once you start looking at this period of British gangs, it's not long before you find the successful 1935 novel about the Glasgow gangs, *No Mean City*. It sometimes goes that novels can be more truthful in establishing a context and a vibe than mere newspaper articles, and that not only made *No Mean City* a wild success commercially, but it earned the wrath of the local population for being a little too honest. Just because the characters were made up did not mean that people could not recognize their neighbours, if not themselves, in the portrayal of interwar Glasgow and its problems.

One of the keys to the book's success is surely that it felt real, and that is because it began life in the mind of a local Gorbals man, Alexander McArthur, who had written a series of novels about real life in Glasgow. McArthur's writing caught the eye of Longmans in London, but they felt the book was not quite ready. Their solution was to send an established London journalist up to Glasgow to meet McArthur. H. Kingsley Long read the manuscript, jumped on a train and struck up a relationship with McArthur. After more meetings, it was agreed that the two men would collaborate on a new story along the lines of the earlier ones. The public response was immediate and not completely positive. This apparently made-up story was just a little too real for many, and in my third printing of the novel there is a defensive authors' preface in which they point out that all great cities have their problems, they are representing just one part of life in an outwardly harmonious city of empire, and that no other city is doing more to improve conditions and re-house citizens as Glasgow.

Belfast

On Saturday, 3 March 1934, the *Irish Weekly and Ulster Examiner* reported that a group of boys had formed into two gangs the previous November, and it was in March when they came before the courts. Ten of the boys had organized themselves into the Half Bap Gang and the The Squealers for the purposes of breaking and entering shops. The gangs would steal sweets and other low value items from shops and then store them in derelict houses around Belfast. The judge commented on one particular detail of the case: that one gang had discovered where

A photo of several leading gangsters taken in 1919, before they all fell out with each other. Thanks to expert author Brian McDonald for confirming the names. Those on the coach (back row) from left to right are bookmaker Claud Fraser, George Hatfield, George Hatfield, Joe Sabini, unknown, unknown, John Gilbert, Harry Sabini, Al Scasini, Brummagem leader Billy Kimber and Bert McDonald. Those standing in the front row from left to right are the charabanc driver, unknown, unknown, Wal McDonald, Billy Endelson, Brian's father Jim McDonald, Tom McDonald, Enrico 'Harry' Cortesi, unknown, unknown, Billy Banks, George Cortesi, Bert Banks, Charles 'Wag' McDonald, Charles 'Darby' Sabini, charabanc assistant. (*Brian McDonald*)

RIVAL BETTING GANGS' AMAZING CHARABANC BATTLE.

Mr. W. Harris, who was injured by roughs in the road battle. Seven people were taken to hospital.

The scene of the amazing charabanc battle between two betting gangs.

An identification parade outside Kingston Police Station in connection with an affray between London and Birmingham betting gangs, which broke out on the road from Epsom. Firearms, axes and hatchets are said to have been used. Arrests on an extensive scale were afterwards made by the "Flying Squad" from Scotland Yard.

Details of a violent fight that began after what seems to have been a deliberate crash between vehicles of rival gangs, *Daily Mirror*, 4th June 1921.

Charabanc outing circa 1920s. (*Adobe Stock*)

East Parade at Worthing, 1922. (*Adobe Stock*)

Charabancs near the pier at Eastbourne East Sussex. Date: 1925. (*Adobe Stock*)

A young Alice Diamond taken from a rare locket or wallet photo discovered in Bert McDonald's Great War diary. (*Brian McDonald*)

SUPPLEMENT A

No. 14.   FRIDAY, JULY 8, 1921.   Vol. VIII.

247 248
249 250
251 252

Alice Diamond of the Forty Thieves shown in a 1921 police file; Alice is image no. 252, bottom right. (*Courtesy of the National Archive*)

Florrie Holmes of the Forty Thieves, once arrested for collecting bets for Bert McDonald. (*Brian McDonald*)

Alf Solomon. (*Brian McDonald*)

Billy Kimber as a young man. (*Brian McDonald*)

WRITTEN
EXCLUSIVELY
for
"THE PEOPLE"

EASY MONEY

as it is obtained by the Spurious and Felonious

MEN-ABOUT-TOWN.

Josephine O'Dare "Blows the Gaff" on a Sinister Phase of West-End Life.

CARUSO.

LIVING IN HER PARK-ST. FLAT.

NO RESPECT FOR WOMEN.

TO FASCINATE THE PRINCE.

SCULPTOR GETS ANGRY.

CREDIT WAS FATALLY EASY.

Josephine O'Dare sample article from *The People*, 17 August 1930 "Easy Money". *(Courtesy of the British Library Board)*

Josephine reached Court all right—but it was a Court which put her in a position where she had years to think over her follies. And she doesn't think these years entirely wasted.

Josephine O'Dare 'Happiness Always Eluded Me,' *The People*, 24 August 1930. (*Courtesy British Library Board*)

Picture of the Sabinis and Cortesis in 1920. Darby Sabini, standing, to the right of the man sitting wearing the boater hat, who is Harry Cortesi. (*Creative Commons*)

The Griffin public house which was the headquarters of the Sabini gang. (*Creative Commons*)

Dartmoor prison from the air, 1953
Atholl, Justin, *Prison on the Moor: the Story of Dartmoor Prison*. (*J. Long, London, 1953*)

Chapel of a civil prison hulk ship, 1846
Johnson, W. Branch (William Branch), *The English Prison Hulks.* (*C. Johnson, 1957*)

Kate Meyrick with friends
Bobbie and Irene in Monte
Carlo, 1931
Meyrick, Kate, *Secrets of the
43: Reminiscences by Mrs.
Meyrick.* (*J. Long, 1933*)

Elephant & Castle. (*Adobe Stock*)

Epsom racecourse 1929. (*Adobe Stock*)

Grand National results via wireless, 1930s. (*Adobe Stock*)

Bookmakers 1929. (*Adobe Stock*)

Ascot horse racing 1839. (*Adobe Stock*)

Cup Day at Ascot 1914. (*Adobe Stock*)

Front view of Bow Street, London 1837. Unknown author, *The Penny Magazine*. (*Adobe Stock*)

Wilmington Swing Bridge, Hull, was opened in 1907 and carried the railway to Hull through its industrial heartland. (*Adobe Stock*)

SHEFFIELD SMOKE.
From a *Drawing by* A. MORROW.

Sheffield Smoke by A Morrow, around 1884. (*Adobe Stock*)

Shadows of the evening steal across the sky   S. 4

Industry – Factories. Date: early 20th century. (*Adobe Stock*)

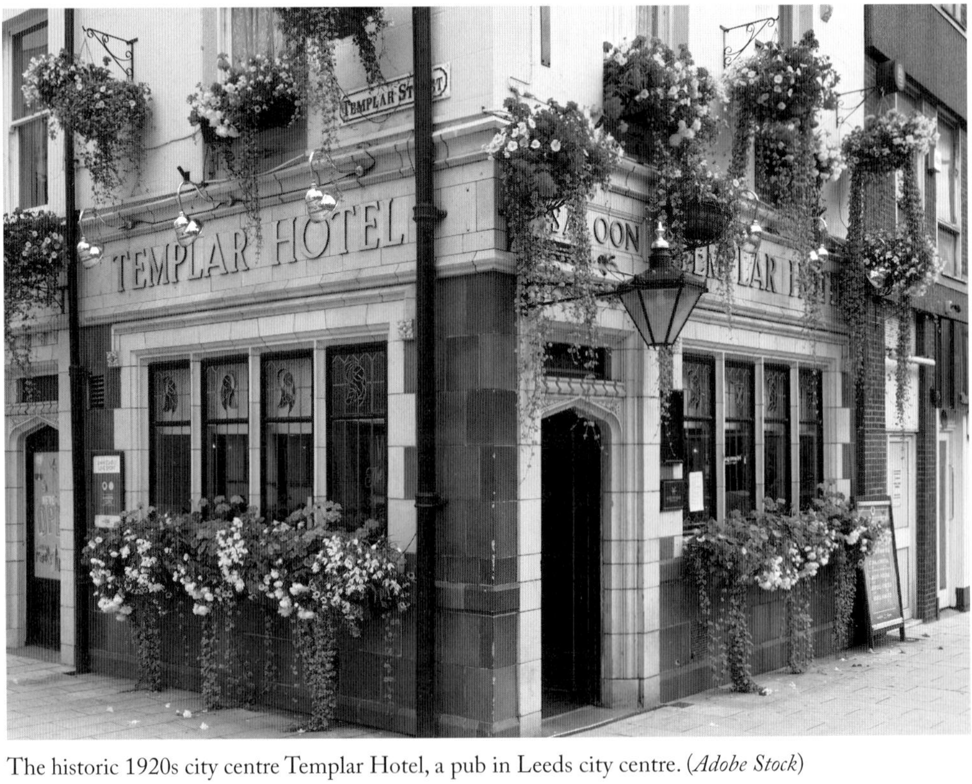

The historic 1920s city centre Templar Hotel, a pub in Leeds city centre. (*Adobe Stock*)

the other stored their stolen goods and stole them from the other gang. The total value of stolen goods was estimated at between £40 and £50 only. All the teenaged boys were placed on probation, and one of them claimed to have been inspired by American movies to steal. The most striking detail of this case was not the young age of the defendants but that a detective had to protect them from being flogged by one of the boy's fathers. It seems likely that the boys feared corporal punishment at home more than the courts. Certainly one aspect of their offending, especially given the small value of stolen goods, was boredom.

Some older, unrelated defendants were sentenced the same day, themselves no strangers to the court, and received a few months' prison with hard labour. This was for offences such as breaking and entering and stealing cigarettes.

The 4 December 1935 edition of the *Belfast Telegraph* covered the annual summary of activity in local courts. The judge noted that Belfast gangs had begun to operate beyond the city and drew attention to threatening letters sent by gang members, especially to households in County Down, demanding that certain occupants or servants should be turned out. From evidence elsewhere it is presumed, but not stated, that those recommended for turning out were Catholics. It was a cowardly act, and recognized as such in law because the standard punishment was penal servitude, even for the act of sending a letter.

Dublin

Our adventure with the British gangs has parallels all over the world but the gangs of Dublin bear special attention. Big sporting events continued for longer in Ireland, which meant gambling and horse racing could continue almost until the end of the war. Many enterprising British gangsters therefore dodged the war draft and moved their activities to Ireland. Another reason for considering Ireland at this time is that the country was gripped by the Home Rule movement. If poverty and crime go together, so do social upheavals and crime. The Home Rule movement of the late nineteenth century culminated in the Home Rule Act, which was signed in 1914, just after the Great War began. These timings were not coincidental. When great change is in the air, an act of parliament is still just a piece of paper. Real change on the ground would take several more years or even decades. Implementation of the new act was at once suspended until the war was over. The anger caused by this delay, after decades of campaigning, can be imagined. Tensions over Home Rule contributed in part to the horrific Easter rebellion of 1916 and the consequences of that dark chapter caused a rise in support for more radical groups than the Home Rule movement, of which one group was Sinn Féin, although a different entity unrelated to today's party of the same name. This is the context in which Ireland began the 1920s.

There is a period of time during which every major British city claims to have the worst slums in Europe. The tenements of Glasgow are a notorious image from this time, but all the other cities we have looked at have their areas of poverty. There were tenement slums in Dublin too, and Kevin C. Kearns, in his detailed study called *Dublin Tenement Life* found that the 1930s were the low point for Dublin's poor. An *Irish Press* article of 1936 proclaimed exactly that: the dilapidated tenements deserved the title 'worst slums in Europe' during that decade. To give an idea of the lead-up to the post-war period, an estimated one-third of Dublin's population lived in tenement buildings, numbering 6,000. By 1938, there were still 6,307 listed tenement houses in the city. To twist the knife further, many of these huge houses had once been the grand city dwellings of the upper classes. They had long since abandoned the country as their property values slumped in favour of more stable places such as America and Britain. As if squalor and hunger were not punishment enough, some of the buildings were so decayed that they would collapse and kill the inhabitants at a moment's notice. What stands out from Kearns' work is his approach. He uses the method of taking oral histories. We can get no closer to the lives of the inhabitants of these tenements than by reading their own words. Even better, much of the testimony was taken in retrospect while the survivors of the slums were still alive, which means there are tape recordings of their voices as well. This guards against something this book is also guarding against: nostalgia. We are not to think that events of a century ago were necessarily glamorous. Yet there is some evidence that, despite the appalling conditions, the residents did manage to achieve a level of contentment with the support of their neighbours. It is a lesson in the power of community to offset almost any deficit in home comforts, or even the necessities of life.

A key area of Dublin at this time that has stuck in the folklore of the period was the Monto. Named after a vanished street called Montgomery Street, the Monto could be found towards the north-east of Dublin in the area known today as Summerhill. The Monto is often labelled dismissively as the red-light district of Dublin for almost a century from 1860 to 1950. Such simple labels hide a fascinating human story in the Monto. We learn from Kearns that many of the Monto sex workers were unmarried young mothers who had been cast aside by their male partners and even their own families. Any study of Ireland at this time must consider not only the political context but also the religious context. The women who came to the Monto from the countryside were not sex workers when they arrived. They had exhausted all other means to support their children and they were typically devout Catholics. The girls were never referred to in derogatory terms in the Monto itself. Even the word brothel was not used. The establishments were instead called 'kips' and the madams were therefore 'kip-keepers'. Meanwhile the sex workers themselves were known for their generosity, despite their own straitened circumstances. Kearns records stories of them giving large tips to messenger boys and even buying shoes for the poorer children who could not afford them.

One of the most striking accounts found by Kearns is the hospital treatment of the women who contracted syphilis. At the time it was incurable and would lead to an inexorable, slow and painful death. One of Kearns' witnesses, Billy Dunleavy, recalls how staff at the hospital would occasionally smother the worst sufferers, a form of euthanasia that still excites strong debate. To say that these were hard times is too simplistic. The oral histories bring the grimness to life.

Some of the accounts from the Dublin tenements confirm what we have seen elsewhere: that nearly all men could defend themselves in a fight without resorting to weapons. Many of them attended boxing clubs and even took part in formal boxing bouts. This would explain the lack of guns, amongst other factors, but also the relative lack of knife attacks. They were so competent with their hands that using a knife was a sign of weakness. This according to Timmy Kirwan, known to all simply as Duck Egg. The unwritten rules of the neighbourhoods placed a high price on honour and pride. But Duck Egg does clarify that the rules of head-to-head fighting and boxing were quite different to what he calls 'gang warfare'. In this, weapons were used, but he does not explicitly say that these weapons were as lethal as knives. One can imagine bottles, bricks and other items coming readily to hand in the tenements. These events were more like mass brawls featuring possibly a dozen or more men. People were sometimes killed; the police were afraid to intervene due to the level of violence and lack of mercy when the gang got into full attack. Gang members would need stitches in head wounds if they survived. They willingly went to hospital to receive stitches, but they could not return to have them removed as the police would wait for them there. So, they removed their own stitches at home with needles.

There were handy hints to self-preservation. Keep a wall behind you so that any attack had to come from in front, where you could see what was happening. And keep your coat on. That way, if someone springs a knife on you, your clothes protect from glancing cuts. This advice was passed on verbally around the streets.

Duck Egg explains that he was one of the youngest members of the gang and makes it clear that when growing up in that neighbourhood, seeing the violence and gang activity led inexorably to the youngsters following their older friends and brothers. As shown in the various academic studies, violence was passed on through the generations easily.

Being strong in number, the gang members were not usually afraid of taking on the police in the area. But some police officers did have the upper hand. Although they all carried batons, and the Dublin Metropolitan police did not carry guns, a few detectives had access to guns at certain times. Duck Egg suggests these were seldom fired but used more as heavy weapons for hitting. The deterrent effect must have been extreme as most gang members preferred fist fights and informal weapons, so the sound of a single gunshot could disperse a large crowd.

Although Dublin had its share of drinking establishments and brothels, it had the most poetic names of all of the cities. The kip houses were brothels with alcohol available. If a place had only drink, it was a shebeen or a speakeasy, which matches with the American word. These were different from the pubs because you could get a drink after hours. There was something illicit about the speakeasies and shebeens which did not apply to the regular pubs. Drink would be hidden anywhere nearby, perhaps in a manhole, ready for the nighttime revels. Strong spirits like whiskey were preferred because they took up less space than drinks like beer. As we have seen elsewhere, especially in London, the police were not only aware of these venues but were also customers. They would take bribes of various kinds to turn a blind eye, as Kate Meyrick found when she entered this world in Soho. Next morning, the men full of drink, the odd fistfight would begin. The police would also fight. It seems that fighting was a regular part of life even for the men who did not align with a gang, and such skills and fitness need continual practice to stay sharp.

The tenements of Dublin were also neighbourhoods of intense bonds and kindness. When Alice Cauldfield lost both of her parents at the age of twelve, Alice, her brother and their four sisters were looked after by neighbours to avoid the family unit being separated. Alice herself would sometimes steal bananas or potatoes to stave off hunger, but she continued to grow up with her siblings in the same streets. Tragically, disease was never far away, and all of Alice's sisters would succumb to tuberculosis, one of the diseases, like cholera and diphtheria, that stalked the poorer areas of all major cities. Such is the value of these oral histories, they really bring out the tiny details that make a life real, whether happy or distressing. Diphtheria would later catch up with Alice, causing a long stay at the Cork Street Hospital.

If anyone was in doubt about the drawbacks of gang life perhaps not being sufficiently serious to deter the idle youth, it was not the leniency of the courts to blame. Johnny Campbell recalls how a month in prison was the typical penalty just for being caught aggressive when drunk. He recalls a neighbour getting a five-year stretch for stealing a jar of sweets from a shop. Johnny himself went away for three years for breaking into a pub. The police were very tough and would be keen to use their batons. As we have found, they would turn a blind eye when it suited them in return for a bribe, but when they were in the mood, they would be violent and strict. One ingenious way to avoid a beating from the police was to feign sickness, which forced them to find a doctor or hospital and prevented them from further injuring the prisoner.

Although the gang members would sometimes use knives, the fights were mainly one-on-one with strict rules. Men would strip to the waist and remove their shoes. Kicking was strictly forbidden. It seems that weapons were more commonly used in the large brawls, which could see twenty men fighting with razor blades, iron bars, flick knives and knuckle-dusters, and even industrial equipment such as large baling hooks they took from the docks. The women would get into disagreements too, typically over the care of children, and sometimes because a mother had hit another's child. They did not stoop to formal weapons, but there is a story Johnny tells of the women using shawls to hit people across the face. The shawls could cut and might even blind the victim.

Close inspection of the Dublin tenements of this period reinforces the complexity of everyday life. Faced with extremes of poverty, the neighbourhood strengthens its bonds. People go out of their way to help others, even when they might themselves be going short of the daily necessities. A striking number of witnesses say how happy they were, living in those crumbling buildings which sometimes collapsed without warning. They were structurally unsound yet spotlessly clean.

There are unexpected distinctions to be drawn between one-on-one street fights, in which weapons were not used and there were very strict codes of conduct, and on the other hand the mass brawls during which it seemed there were no rules at all, and people might occasionally be killed. This was a varied, contrasting and surprising microcosm. Although it is clear that poverty did breed crime and gang behaviour, those subscribing to a gang were still in a minority. Most people just wanted to get on with survival, apart from the routine scuffle outside the pub on a Friday night, which in some senses was just a way to maintain their survival instincts. Perhaps poverty is essential as a foundation for the gangs, but personality and other circumstances are important too.

We can place Billy Kimber in Dublin in the spring of 1917. By this time he had signed up and deserted from the army fighting the Great War. Horse racing was fully closed down in Britain but not in Ireland. Dublin was calling.

The *Daily Express* of 4 May introduces us to Kimber's antics and the same paper on 11 May 1917 explores some of the repercussions of Kimber's arrival in Dublin. The headline 'Alleged Pocket-Picking' gives the gist of what happened. Kimber is inexplicably described as a china dealer, which gives us cause to wonder if this is the same William Kimber of Peaky Blinders fame. It is, of course, and his address is given as 17 New Cut, Lambeth, London as well as 20 Mountjoy Street, Dublin. His co-conspirator was a man called James Cope, whose address was also given as 20 Mountjoy Street. The two men stood accused of pickpocketing around Kingsbridge Station in Dublin on the morning of a Limerick horse race meeting, 3 May 1917. They were also accused of undertaking the same offence at Harcourt station on the morning of racing at Leopardstown, 27 April and at Sackville Street on 1 May. Thomas Henry Day, a Bond Street bookmaker, had employed Kimber as a debt collector at the races and was prepared to stand bail for his employee. Bail for both men was set at £50 but there was a twist in the tail for Kimber, and a detail that confirms him to be the William Kimber of interest to us. He was charged with being a deserter from the Army Service Corps since 11 June 1915 and remanded into custody to await a military escort. A similar article, though slightly shorter, confirmed these details in the *Freeman's Journal* of the same date, 11 May 1917.

The more detailed *Daily Express* article from 4 May includes some testimony heard in court. Witnesses placed the accused, Kimber and Cope, at various race meetings in the company of various men, some of them known Dublin pickpockets. This therefore means the 11 May articles recount the hearings at the end of their one-week remand period. Unfortunately for our purposes, Kimber's hearing subsequent to 11 May in relation to his army desertion is not recorded in the *Daily Express*.

Although these articles cover only one brief episode in Billy Kimber's Irish sojourn, they do not portray him as a violent criminal mastermind. In the eyes of Irish justice, Kimber has a spotless record and is described as a china dealer of good standing, even though all of the testimony relates to his work as a racecourse debt collector from London. Mention of his army desertion dispels any slim possibility that this might have been a different William Kimber of Lambeth, London.

Chapter 7

America

I wanted to include a short section on America because its gangsters were often compared to British gangs in the newspapers, and several of them were so famous that they were featured in Hollywood movies and are remembered to this day.

A 1930 novel called *Scarface* became a 1932 movie and a 1983 remake. In the 1983 version, perhaps the most famous one, Al Pacino took the lead role of Tony Montana. But it was the earlier 1932 movie that caused a sensation among British youth of the time, and many of the sources I used to research British gang violence in the period pointed to *Scarface* as a negative influence. The 1932 movie was certainly popular at a time when cinema was becoming the dominant cultural phenomenon. The movies are only loosely based on the original novel by long-forgotten author Armitage Trail, one of the many pen-names of Maurice R. Coons. The book and original movie were set in Chicago, which Trail knew well, whereas the 1983 remake by Brain DePalma moved the action to Miami. *Scarface* and his only other novel, *The Thirteenth Guest*, demonstrate that Trail could have become one of the century's most famous crime writers had he not died suddenly of a heart attack at the age of twenty-eight, before the movie of his book was finished. Weighing in at over three hundred pounds, Trail was dangerously obese. Fittingly, his heart failed in the Paramount Theatre in Los Angeles.

The most pertinent feature of *Scarface* is that the lead character is loosely based on everyone's most famous gangster, Al Capone. Al Capone is so famous that he is known to everyone, even those who don't watch gangster movies or have any interest in gangs. His fame seems to stem from two factors: he was wildly successful financially, and his influence on the Chicago crime scene was vast. He was never brought to justice for his gang antics, even though he ordered hits on his rivals, but was finally put in prison for tax evasion. Capone's story mirrors many of the tales from Britain about how youngsters got involved in crime. Although his family was quite poor, Capone was doing reasonably well at school in New York and was certainly not involved in crime. He failed sixth grade, and it seems that his life started to go off track at that point. He had a violent physical altercation with a teacher and never returned to school. This combination of lack of stimulation and poverty is always risky and Capone began hanging around at the docks. It was a chance meeting with a gang leader, Johnny Torrio, that finally set Capone on the road to crime; just as in *Scarface*, our comparatively staid and fresh-faced hero is led astray by older gang leaders. Capone earned his nickname, 'Scarface', when he was attacked by a man with a knife that left three permanent scars on his cheeks.

Al Capone's life returned to normality when he married at the age of nineteen and had a child, Albert Francis. The Capones relocated to Baltimore and he got an ordinary job, temporarily leaving the life of crime behind him. In another example of how difficult it could be to go straight, Torrio got in touch with Capone after Capone's father died and invited the family to Chicago to help Torrio run a massively successful organized crime operation. Several generations of the Capone family followed Al to Chicago and he quickly cemented his reputation as the city's greatest ever gangster during the enormously lucrative prohibition years. His ambition knew no limits and this ultimately led to his downfall. He had seven rivals killed in a single day on the St Valentine's Day massacre of 1929 and the authorities decided to strike. Although they failed to catch him for organizing the assassinations, the federal government, on the personal instruction of US President Herbert Hoover, began to prosecute Capone for tax evasion. He was sent down for a relatively short stretch but was switched to Alcatraz after two years. His health declined as he developed dementia caused by syphilis, and he was released to a mental hospital in Baltimore before the end of his eleven-year sentence.

Capone's career is shadowed by the fictional protagonists in the various versions of *Scarface*, but it is also shadowed throughout Britain and America. Perhaps, as with any legitimate career, a particular combination of aptitude, opportunity and finding the right (or wrong) mentors at a vulnerable time enabled Al Capone to rise beyond the heights in wealth and reputation of any other gangster of his era. That he is immortalized in two well-received movies and still spoken of today perhaps gives some indication of just how notorious his activities were by the time he was finally brought to justice. The only surprise is that he was a more-or-less ordinary family man when he was not having his rivals and innocent bystanders killed.

George Clarence 'Bugs' Moran is partly the inspiration for the musical spoof *Bugsy Malone*. It was members of his gang who were shot dead during the St Valentine's Day massacre perpetrated by Al Capone. The massacre is also a key plot point in *Scarface*, a film which is mentioned in many of the sources reporting on British gangs between the wars. It was released just before the formal introduction of the Hollywood code which clipped the wings of producers and studios in terms of what sexual and violent content could be shown onscreen. Even in the absence of those rules, significant changes were requested, including the inclusion at the start of some frames of text which condemn violence and describe the film as a cautionary tale. The ending was also changed to punish the protagonist more severely, although modern audiences are normally shown the original. Recent digital downloads of the movie are shown in a square frame, which always reduces the impact of films made for cinema. There is virtually no incidental music at all, which somehow adds to the impact because it is unusual. And due to its history the film still qualifies for an '18' rating in the UK. Yet there is no gore, no bad language, no sexual content, virtually all of the shootings are shown from a distance and, memorably, the shooting that opens the movie is performed behind a closed blind in silhouette. The fist-fighting scenes are so poorly produced as to be almost slapstick. Yet, to imagine ourselves sitting in a 1930s cinema, perhaps having fought in the Great War and anxious about a new war yet to come, with these hoodlums up on a giant screen in front of a packed, hushed house, it is just about possible to imagine its influence on the young minds present. There are the wisecracking one-liners that became a hallmark of American pulp fiction. Easy to imagine the kids of Glasgow and Birmingham repeating these lines endlessly in their playgrounds and yards. It is easy to see how this film was successful at the time and is still talked about today. But quite difficult to imagine it provoking anyone to pick up a gun and start shooting. In the 1980s, computer games went through a similar phase we could describe as pre-code. The graphics were so rudimentary that nobody thought to censor or edit the games for violence. We shot each other up with the most appalling weapons, and not one friend turned to crime as a result. I can remember no news headlines, however sensationalist, from those early computer game years, claiming that the games had caused a violent event. It is ridiculous to blame *Scarface* and various copycat movies for turning British youth, or even American youth, into gangsters.

Scarface did cause controversy on its release, and it was censored, even in the absence of a formal Hollywood code. But Robert E. Sherwood got close to the truth when he said that the authorities tried to suppress the movie only because it was too truthful, not because it was too violent. Precisely the same comments were made about the earlier Glasgow novel *No Mean City*. People turned against it not because it was a bad book, but because it was too accurately reflecting real life in the city. In the context of its time, it was too painful to read. *Scarface* exposed the wanton violence that is the most eye-catching aspect of organized crime, suggesting that prohibition itself caused the racketeering (and later historians have shown that it did) and, therefore, it simply had to be silenced. This can happen when entertainment grows too large for its fedora hat: if people start to think fiction is non-fiction, they start to become more critical and less tolerant. Escapism is only acceptable for the masses if it is escapist, not if it hits home and makes people question the status quo, the very fabric of society. No, *Scarface* did not turn Glasgow youth to violence. The violence was already present, it was just hushed up.

Chicago

All accounts of gangland America start in Chicago with the life of Al Capone. He is the archetype against which we compare every gangster since, anywhere in the Western world. Why does Al remain so famous today?

Capone was ruthless. The fear he instilled in other gangsters, law enforcement and anyone in a position of authority was real. This led to him gaining sweeping powers over the judiciary and politicians across Chicago and beyond. He didn't overstretch. He stayed out of California and New York, for example. He must have been charming when he needed to be, and, paradoxically for someone so violent, he was also fair-minded. This picture of Capone emerges from the excellent 1971 biography of Capone by John Kobler, which remains the benchmark life of Al Capone today. Written just twenty-five years after Capone's death, it was long enough after the event to catch some perspective, but close enough that Capone's shadow still lingered. It would have been comparatively easy for Kobler to imagine his way into 1920s Chicago. A biographer coming to the same topic today has no hope of conjuring up the desperate poverty faced by immigrant Italian families. Capone himself, as he repeatedly reminded everyone, was born in Brooklyn, but his father was born in Naples, not Sicily, which was to become synonymous with the American Mafia. Perhaps this combination of chances helped Capone's notoriety: he did not dissolve into the Sicilian crime scene which was so large and sprawling that its interconnected webs stretched across the entire United States. The Neapolitan families were not that successful at crime. So Capone stood out: he seemed Italian, not American, and to the Italians he was from Naples, not Sicily. He didn't fit into any slot and had to make his own. Kobler feels the need to let us know how Capone is pronounced, which would not be necessary in a book written now. The original Italian name was Caponi, so the changed pronunciation was important in making the family sound less Italian, even though their strong accents would have given the game away in any conversation.

Most of them had very poor English and were illiterate, and their only skills were in agriculture which were useless in the loud, chaotic mean streets of Brooklyn. They got the most menial and physically demanding jobs for less money than the American locals. An honest Italian immigrant, taking one of these jobs as a bricklayer or stonecutter, was condemned to a life of poverty. A man's wife would have had to work too at a time when a middle class American family would expect the woman of the house to raise the children. Even the children of the Brooklyn slums had to work from a young age, just as they did in Britain. The New York tenements were every bit as disgusting as the British ones, with only cold water if there was running water, poor sanitation and insufficient light and air. The youth were so unhealthy they were rejected for military service, just as the inner-city teenagers in Britain were also rejected. Too unfit even to be slaughtered on the Somme, no wonder that for a tiny minority of the boys, their minds turned to more creative ways to get by.

The methods used by the Italian community were highly creative. They were born out of a unique history and set of circumstances. They didn't merely copy the methods of the Mafia, and related societies such as the Camorra from Naples, or the Carbonari. They blended those ideas with the methods of American capitalism, thereby turning the local business community against itself like a trojan horse. When prohibition arrived, they suddenly had something to sell that was highly profitable and they applied the methods of Henry Ford to moonshine. Combining Italian ingenuity and American mass production turned out to be as profitable as the Silicon Valley tech industry was to become half a century later.

As with the Soho nightclubs in London, Chicago's organized crime needed a meeting place, a venue to while away the long nights drinking and dancing. For Al Capone, the main venue was always Colosimo's Café, named for James 'Big Jim' Colismo, although his real name was Vincenzo. It had the best chefs, the best wines, the best musicians and the prettiest girls. The whole place shone in its own light against the drab realities of 1920s' Chicago. The place was famous across America and attracted all the main celebrities of the day, including sports stars, academics, journalists, movie stars and everyone in between, including gangsters. This, too, was mirrored in London: the gangsters went where the mainstream stars were, and, tellingly, the mainstream stars accepted them. They were not afraid. They had no reason to be, as long as they didn't ask too many questions or look at someone the wrong way. Colisimo was a fearless and successful gangster in his own right, and died after being shot by his deputy, John 'The Fox' Torrio. Torrio was also an associate of Capone, and although the trigger was pulled by Frankie Yale, who had travelled from New York specifically to shoot Colisimo, both Torrio and Capone were implicated in the assassination. Colisimo's mistake was to resist the bootlegging profits made possible by the newly-arrived prohibition laws, and his once-trusted henchman lost patience with him. Gangsters settled disputes in the quickest way they knew.

The death of Al Capone's father back home in Brooklyn came as a great shock. Gabriel Capone was just fifty-two when he died of a heart attack brought on by myocarditis. After the funeral, Al immediately set about moving his closest family members over to Chicago and housing them near him. The only exception was his eldest brother, Jim, with whom they had lost touch. When funds allowed, he even had his father's remains exhumed and reburied in Mount Olivet Cemetery in Chicago. The Capone blood ran thick, as it did in all of the expatriate Italian families.

Although Al Capone was still establishing his crime business, and still building his fearsome reputation, he had the funds to prepare well for his mother's arrival. Teresa Capone moved into a fifteen-room redbrick house on South Prairie Avenue, no. 7244. The interior decor was sumptuous, including gilded cornices and huge mirrors. The bathroom fittings were from Germany and the walls were reinforced against bullets.

Al Capone's myth as the most notorious gangster in modern American history, at least to non-gang buffs, is never balanced against his unbreakable family bonds. He looked after his relatives way beyond what might be considered a normal filial duty, and he was mostly loyal to his trusted deputies and associates. Yet he was capable of sudden, extreme and sadistic violence when the need arose. He wasn't afraid to use his strength or any weapons to hand. The more you dig into the histories of the gangsters, the more you find they have a lot in common with the rest of us, only more so.

To close this section on Chicago, an article reported in the *Belfast Telegraph* on 23 May 1930 shows how newspapers collaborated and shared content in ways familiar with today's readers. The *London Express* provided the *Belfast Telegraph* with horrific details of a story from the Chicago underworld. After a bundle of human bones was found, the Chicago police leapt to an assumption that perhaps underworld gangsters had started cremating their victims to destroy evidence. As the paper drily admits, 'there is no evidence to support this theory'. The most obvious question is why the bones themselves were not cremated with the rest of the victims although, at the time, techniques to identify victims from bones did not exist. The theory seems to have taken root after the bones were found in woods near to an underworld hideout. The bones were believed to belong to Benny Bennett, a gambler who had been close with Al Capone. Another gangster affiliated with Capone, George Higgins, had also recently disappeared without trace. Although there might be no evidence for the cremation theory, the police were clearly treating the idea seriously and it would explain why a clean pile of bones was found in the woods.

Los Angeles

If Al Capone is the only gangster famous among the general public, even outside America, then Jack Dragna is often introduced as the Capone of Los Angeles. Unlike Capone, Dragna really was Italian. Born as Ignazio Dragna in Corleone, Sicily in 1891, he arrived in Brooklyn with a few family members at a tender age, in 1898, a year before Al Capone was born. They were growing up in the same communities in Brooklyn at the same time. This is significant because it means that all the hardships faced by the Italian immigrant communities were felt by both young boys. After ten years in the US, Dragna returned to Sicily. Dragna returned to Brooklyn in 1914 but fled after being linked with the murder of Barnet Baff. He wasn't tried for the Baff murder but he was jailed for extortion. It was on his release that he started using the name Jack Dragna. It was 1931 before Dragna rose to prominence in the Los Angeles underworld, taking over the helm of the LA crime family from Joseph Ardizzone, who had disappeared in mysterious circumstances. As with the death of Big Jim implicating Capone, many suspected Dragna was involved in Ardizzone's murder. No doubt Dragna is more famous in the US than overseas. He appeared in James Ellroy's successful *LA Quartet* novels.

The British Arrive

The British gangs were successful right up to the Second World War. Like any successful business, they decided to branch out overseas in the early 1920s. Wag McDonald jumped on a boat and set sail for a new world, in Canada. The boat took him right into the heart of North America: Quebec.

Wag made it to the city of Los Angeles in 1923, which then had a very new and thriving feel, even though it had been established as a city as early as 1781 and there had been a settlement on the site since 1542 when the Spanish bought the land. The impetus in the city that

Wag knew had been provided by modern transportation. The railway arrived from New Orleans in 1876 followed by the Santa Fé in 1885. In 1892, oil was discovered in the area and a new form of gold rush began. Wag's diaries talk of Hollywood as a movie town, and of it being separate from the city of Los Angeles when he first saw it. So this electric combination of comfortable, fast transport and movie-star glamour caused a boom. Los Angeles was the Las Vegas of the 1920s, and Wag arrived at the perfect moment.

There was only one cloud in Wag's Los Angeles sky: prohibition. For years, a movement had been building in America to outlaw alcohol. Unbelievable to Europeans then, as now, it was one of those crackpot ideas that made sense to a lot of people at the time and, in 1919, the US states together ratified the 18th Amendment which prohibited everything connected with alcohol except drinking it: banned were the manufacture, sale and transportation of all intoxicating liquors but, of course, there is only one intoxicating liquor. Import and export was also banned, which prevented entrepreneurs smuggling the stuff in from Mexico or Canada. There was one other loophole, apart from it being still legal to drink booze, and it was that the ban did not extend to industrial alcohol production for purposes other than drinking. It was not until 1933 that America came to its senses and passed the 21st Amendment, bringing prohibition to a close. What was an outlaw like Wag to do, other than to turn this situation into a business opportunity?

Jack Dragna was just getting going at this time. He had in mind vague notions of copying the model of the Chicago mobs in Los Angeles and set about building his own mob. He is widely regarded as the head of all the Los Angeles organized crime networks at that time, even though he was only thirty. It takes quite some imagination to appreciate this achievement. Think of all the scrapes, brawls and near-death experiences of the London gangs and you get a good idea of the danger that Dragna had navigated. Yes, he was in Los Angeles at the right time, but so were countless others. Dragna had the magic stardust.

In his excellent book *Elephant Boys*, Brian McDonald describes Wag as a 'strong arm' man for Dragna who also worked as his accountant. His role was to look after the money in the widest possible sense, including the forceful collection of debts. This was a fortuitous decision for Wag. As a rank outsider, there was no way he could hope to supplant someone with Dragna's established power. And Dragna's boys had a certain exotic presence missing from the raw, violent, rain-soaked London mobs. Dragna's colleagues looked stylish and lived the high life and it is natural that someone with Wag's background joined them. His real achievement though seems to have been to position himself as Dragna's right-hand man. Wag certainly had clout. He lived in rooms next to Dragna's Wilshire Boulevard hotel suite at the Ambassador's. One of their business services, of course, was the illegal selling of alcohol in speakeasies they called 'blind pigs' because the cheap stuff really could cause blindness.

For all Dragna's success, he lacked the ruthlessness of Al Capone. Although far from soft, he was more accommodating of both his men and their customers, which led to plenty of work for Wag in collecting debts. Their main rivals in LA at this time were the Triads, and one day they caught up with Wag in a place known as Ferguson's Alley. Wag was almost stabbed with a long blade, which instead sliced through his bag, and he held the bag up to defend himself against more slashes. His sidekick, Tommy Carroll, a boxer, knocked the Triad to the ground, but it was a close shave. Their getaway car that day was one of those classic 1920s' American automobiles with running boards, and Carroll leaped onto the car as Wag pulled away, gathering speed only slowly, which led to the comical scene of a gang of Triads chasing the car along the street. High danger was never far away from comedy, it seems.

Both Tommy and Wag had a fierce sense of humour for practical trickery and would leave ticking gadgets for Dragna to find. This small detail is telling. Both men had a relationship with Dragna that could be described in two ways: they were relaxed in his company and felt comfortable doing silly tricks, but Jack Dragna's frantic, nervous reaction to these japes is important too. He did not feel secure, and those close to him could get away with playing on his anxieties, partly because they knew that Dragna's entire organization depended on loyal sidekicks like them. He just wasn't terrifying enough on his own to rule by fear alone.

The glamour ran through this gang in other ways. Tommy Carroll shared a name with a famous actress of the time, Nancy Carroll. They were not related, but there was a passing resemblance and joker Tommy would tell people that she was his sister. In a town like LA back then, this little trick was gold dust that served both him and Wag well. Both men ended up with walk-on parts and crowd scenes in successful movies starring Lon Chaney and John Gilbert. That heady mix of crime and show business recurred later in Las Vegas with Frank Sinatra. It is a common thread in modern American history.

While Tommy chased the most eligible actresses of the time, Wag could be found working as a minder for some of the most important male stars. This is how he ran across Charlie Chaplin. It is worth reminding ourselves that Chaplin grew up not only in London, but in Lambeth, the stomping ground of Wag and the Elephant & Castle Boys. It is likely that this shared background was the catalyst they needed to form a relationship. Wag would drive his idol around town to various appointments and parties. Eventually, he became appalled at Chaplin's taste for girls under the legal age, and their relationship soured. Chaplin had also somehow avoided a spell in the war which did not impress a strongman like Wag.

By the end of the 1920s Billy Kimber and Bert McDonald had fled a spicy shoot-out in London to join Wag in Los Angeles. It was planned that way. Billy Kimber travelled first to New York with Bert McDonald. Kimber had arranged to connect with a friend in Arizona and help with his business there. By the time Kimber and Bert arrived, the friend had been shot and the business was closed. Bert took a construction job on the new highway across the Mojave Desert towards Los Angeles and managed to link up with Wag there. But Billy had to beat a retreat when it was discovered he was travelling on a false passport. The woman with him was calling herself Mrs Kimber and her passport was in that name. They were not married either and Billy bolted for Chicago on the Union Pacific railroad with his friend. Once in Chicago, Billy found Murray 'the Camel' Humphreys, who shared a Welsh ancestry with the Kimbers. Humphreys was a senior member of Al Capone's gang and attended Capone's funeral, according to Kobler. Not long after, in August 1929, Kimber was helped to return to London. His frantic time in America with both Jack Dragna and Al Capone had tested his nerves but, by gang standards of the time, he was getting on, at the ripe age of forty-seven.

Bonnie and Clyde

There is no better real-life crime couple to illustrate the way fact and fiction blur through the decades. Are they the only crime couple whose first names are sufficient to introduce them?

Bonnie Parker was from a slightly more affluent family than Clyde Barrow, but only just. A diminutive character, standing barely five-feet high, she is invariably introduced first. The reason Bonnie and Clyde stand out is due to Bonnie, and the reason she stands out is that she was a woman in a man's world. They were almost the same age and both died together in their middle twenties in a hail of bullets in their car on 23 May 1934. Their story has been distorted in the years since, but I found John Treherne's 1984 book *The Strange History of Bonnie and Clyde* a great read that seeks to dig into the facts, waving aside the Hollywood depictions.

It seems likely that the main reason we remember Bonnie and Clyde today is the incredible 1967 Hollywood movie with two landmark actors. Faye Dunaway was Bonnie and Warren Beatty played Clyde. Perhaps an argument can be made that this film was inspired by the success of 1958's *The Bonnie Parker Story* but I am not convinced. That film title doesn't mention Clyde and the double act, the romantic attachment between the couple, is surely the most compelling feature of their story. Also, nobody today remembers Dorothy Provine who played Bonnie in the earlier film, but Dunaway and Beatty are still gigantic names in Hollywood in the present day.

The emphasis on Bonnie and Clyde obscures the fact that there was a cast of helpers, a group that some sources identify as a gang. This element legitimately makes this group a gang, but it is not the same kind of organization we are familiar with from Britain at this time, which tended to be a larger group of loosely bonded individuals. This was more like a single unit engaged in organized crime or, perhaps, disorganized crime. Clyde Barrow was a candidate for being one of the most calamitously poor burglars in the United States. He was forever making basic errors and getting caught. He spent months in prison and only managed to escape a fourteen-year sentence by some unclear decision of the parole board. On another occasion he escaped using a gun smuggled in by Bonnie, only to be caught just days later. At some point, after one prison release, it seems likely he developed severe mental health problems, possibly including psychopathy. The most likely explanation seems to be that prison exacerbated existing problems. Poverty on its own was not enough to make him one of the twentieth century's best-remembered criminals. It was a combination of poverty, poor mental health, meeting Bonnie, and then the ambush that led to them being shot by over one hundred bullets that made the wider public view these lethal hoodlums as victims.

Bonnie and Clyde were killed in a manner that even the hardest Mafia mobster might baulk at. It was a summary execution, an assassination, in flagrant contravention of the laws and justice system in which America placed its trust. That ambush, by former and serving rangers and sheriffs, perhaps hoping for a reward or, at the very least, public approbation was surely stoked by irresponsible and exaggerated reporting in the local newspapers. The six who planned and carried out the ambush could be described as vigilantes from today's standpoint and had little in common with normal law enforcement practices.

The irresistible cocktail of public pressure, stoked by the newspapers of the time, led to an extremely violent ambush and death but even this was not the end of the story. As word spread of the shocking scenes, vast crowds descended on the small town of Arcadia in Louisiana. The legend of Bonnie and Clyde began on that day. The promised reward never materialized which led to the vigilante posse taking whatever souvenirs they could grab from the car in which Bonnie and Clyde died. In further unsavoury developments, the car containing the bodies of Bonnie and Clyde was mobbed. Bystanders removed hairs from Bonnie's head and scraps of material from her blood-soaked dress. John Treherne claims a man even tried to amputate Clyde's unused trigger finger. Later on, with the bodies inside two different funeral homes, crowds arrived to inspect the corpses. Yet again the police operation was deficient and the authorities had little choice but to let the crowds view the dead gangsters for themselves.

Clyde Barrow's funeral was a similar farce. The pressure of the crowd was so great that some mourners almost fell into the open grave. Bonnie Parker's funeral was more restrained and respectful but her body had not been able to rest at her own home due to the large crowds gathered there. It is clear from the last hours of Bonnie and Clyde, and their aftermath, that the media had stoked public opinion across several counties and beyond. The near-hysterical antics from the local police and the wider public is proof of it.

The electric chair would have awaited the two even if they had faced trial, but at least a proper process would have been followed and the dead gangsters' bodies would not have faced mutilation and mob hysteria. The whole episode discredits everyone involved. It was a mob circus and a mishandled situation. How could Bonnie and Clyde, gangsters who had killed eleven people including nine police officers, begin to look like victims? Only if law enforcement enabled a band of vigilantes to stake out an ambush and then mistreat the possessions and bodies afterwards. It became a David-and-Goliath story that enthralled cinema audiences in 1967 and for years beyond and inspired numerous hit records including a French language song sung by Serge Gainsbourg and Brigitte Bardot. The more famous song, at least in Britain, was Georgie

Fame's lilting musical hall tribute to the gangsters. Its narrative style attempts to convey the key elements of the story in song but its light, jokey melody is in stark contrast to the lives of the real couple.

The profusion of guns owned by Bonnie and Clyde, and the arsenal they faced from the vigilante posse which ended their crime spree, could possibly only have existed in America. It is impossible to imagine a similar scene in Britain where the pistol, never mind the machine gun, was the weapon of the coward. In the end we find that the lives, death and continuing legend of Bonnie and Clyde is a true American crime classic. Their lives were distorted and magnified by disingenuous journalists looking to sell papers, which led to a vigilante posse, and likely more than one, tracking their movements in hopes of a cash reward. The non-payment of the reward led to thefts of evidence and artefacts from the death car which, unsurprisingly, was itself the subject of bitter recriminations.

Once Hollywood got a whiff of the dramatic potential of the story, at just the right remove, safely after the Second World War, when living memories of what actually happened that day were hopelessly confused, things might still have gone wrong. But casting two Hollywood legends in a brilliantly successful movie, full of its own inventions and distortions, that generated spin-off hit singles in several languages, ensured that not only American but Western culture would fondly remember these two over a century after their births.

Chapter 8

Prison Time

Prisons are an important part of the professional criminal's world. Every day, every new enterprise brings with it the risk of being caught or implicated by a colleague or rival. Prisons are an important part of the British cultural psyche too, featuring prominently in Victorian novels by Charles Dickens, and in modern TV series such as Ronnie Barker's *Porridge*. Many of our prisons were built during the Victorian era. Not surprising that many have fallen out of use in recent decades, but slightly surprising that so many of them have become hotels or tourist attractions. But before the Victorians, Britain had no properly-funded organized prison system. The most severe punishments were execution or transportation to the colonies.

Strange then, that so many books about British gangsters and their lives barely even mention the possibility of a stretch behind bars. The heists, the chases and the shoot-outs, the fights and vendettas surely make for better entertainment than stories of prison time, but understanding the prisons of the early twentieth century is vital to a full understanding of the gangs and how they thought. At times when police and the courts are more active, gang activity does seem to ease. At other times when the police were thought to be corruptible, or the prison officers bribable by the inmates, prison could be seen as less of a punishment. There are many stories of key lynchpins conducting their business from within a prison cell. How the criminals themselves view the prospect of prison, and the conditions in our prisons, which were truly appalling during the period we are looking at, are an integral part of how they see the world and themselves within it. Welcome to the chokey.

The Prison Hulk Ships

The ships were a 'temporary' alternative to transportation, intended to be used for one year. The British penal system was convicting so many men, and there were so many crimes punishable by transportation to the colonies – initially America and the Caribbean, later Australia and New Zealand – that the ships could not transport the criminals fast enough or often enough. An alternative solution was urgently needed. William Branch Johnson's excellent 1957 book, *The English Prison Hulks*, is a nicely illustrated account of these times.

Although enforced transportation had been a punishment in English law since 1597, things really warmed up in the late eighteenth century. In the eyes of the British public and justice system, was there anything very much different between shipping someone overseas for years of hard labour, or keeping them in Britain to work on useful public projects? It seems there was at first, because hard labour had only been enforced on those transported to the far reaches of the empire. After the American colonies rebelled in 1775, this transportation system ground to a halt. For the first time, a bill was drafted to allow convicts to carry out manual labour in Britain, digging up hard core and aggregates for building works or, in an oddly specific detail, cleansing the bed of the river Thames.

The Thames was the only waterway into London's sprawling docks, the largest in the world as the empire flourished. Given that one of the jobs for the convicts was to dredge the silted riverbed, what better accommodation for them than a rotting old ship at anchor? An unscrupulous merchant named Duncan Campbell was put in charge of the new system and he appointed his brother Neil as his deputy. The Act of Parliament was finalized in May 1776 and by August groups of convicts were clearing up the river. This solved the problem of the broken transportation system and also provided useful work for the convicts at home. One of their jobs was to construct yards and docks for the Woolwich Arsenal. There were unintended consequences, as always. The word of these gangs of prisoners, toiling in full view of the public, spread quickly and sightseeing parties were arranged to spectate. Criminal punishment had once again become a public spectacle, entertainment for the middle and upper classes. The only remedy was to relocate the working gangs behind a brick wall and the sightseeing stopped, but the newspaper stories continued to entertain.

The convicts usually kept themselves in line because their only hope of early release was to be obedient. Yet there were occasional outbreaks of violence. Some prisoners were shot for causing trouble and fighting with the guards. One afternoon in September 1778 an armed group of perhaps 150 prisoners tried to escape. The captain, who had been tipped off, tried to dissuade the men but they set about attacking him. Missiles flew in the air, and shots were fired. Two of the leaders of the revolt were killed and seven or eight more were seriously injured.

One explanation for the occasional flare up is the appalling conditions on the hulk that served as their hostel. The press frequently attacked the Campbells and the conditions on the hulks. An enquiry found that the system was not as bad as the press claimed, but this was largely because Campbell stuffed the court with his associates and bribed people not to be critical. The reality was the diseases such as typhus and dysentery were rife and the 'hospital' area on the ship was the small forecastle, within which the sick were not separated from the injured. The stench emanating from the area was appalling and disease ripped through the ship. There were no beds at first, and then only straw mattresses on the floor, but the prisoner's leg irons were kept on. Things gradually improved under immense public pressure. The ships were also overcrowded.

All thoughts about them being a temporary solution gradually faded from memory. In a parallel with Kate Meyrick's recollections of Holloway Prison, the diet was terrible on the hulk ships. Boiled ox cheek, which might be made into soup, awful bread and dry biscuits were common staples. The biscuits were often smashed into crumbs and frequently mouldy. On two days of the week, meat was replaced by oatmeal and cheese. Half an ox cheek would feed six men and the cheeks were usually rancid. Small beer was served on four days of the week, and on the other three days foul and badly filtered river water was on offer. The quantity of all this filth was as low as the quality.

By the end of the eighteenth century there was no sign of the hulks being abolished, despite everyone with true knowledge of conditions condemning them. The press and public condemned them and even a 1798 Parliamentary Committee found that released prisoners were even more likely to offend than when they arrived at the start of their hard labour sentence. The ships had become just another colony of sorts, not quite outside the law but somewhat out of sight. Reformers made a strong case for the creation of proper, permanent prisons with proper living conditions that could start the hard work of improving the behaviour of inmates. Excuses were always found not to carry out the plans because the hulks were far cheaper than building proper prisons.

Another commission recommended more modest improvements: perhaps the sick could be moved to another prison ship to stop disease spreading? Perhaps chaplains might help the mood and improve behaviour? Maybe sentences could be shorter? These plans were enacted at various speeds but these investigations did make Campbell and friends think twice. By now, prison ships had appeared at Portsmouth and Plymouth in addition to the originals at Woolwich on the Thames. These ships had more convicts and even worse diets than Woolwich, and not coincidentally were a very long way from London, beyond the reach of influential witnesses. Convicts began dying in larger numbers. A hulk appeared at Sheerness in 1810. The number of ships was increasing and the hulk system was beginning to look permanent.

The hulks became politically useful during the Napoleonic wars. By 1811 there were at least twenty ships holding prisoners of war. How could the nation justify holding military prisoners in a better standard than civilians? The answer was simple: the hulks would remain and grow in number.

Recalling that the prison hulks had been established in 1776 for a period of one year, it might be surprising to learn that they were still in operation in 1847, although in a slightly different form. No longer used for the transportation of criminals, they were more commonly used for any convict deemed unfit for housing in a permanent prison. Another report was taken seriously and the existing regime was brought to an end. Significant improvements were at last made in diet and living conditions. Corporal punishment declined and proper professional management was put in place. However, the end of the hulks was inevitable and in 1848 the prisoners were directed to break up some of the old ships that had incarcerated them. By 1852 a proper permanent prison at Portsmouth was ready. On 14 July 1857 the final ship, the *Defence*, went up in flames. Dartmoor prison had been erected between 1806 and 1809, so there was a considerable period of overlap with the prison hulks.

Dartmoor

Dartmoor has always been famous in Britain for being both beautiful unspoilt countryside and a prison. It is also a vast army training area. Remote areas are typically unspoilt, of course, but also suited to housing dangerous criminals and hosting violent military training exercises. These contradictions might offer a clue as to why Dartmoor grips the nation's culture and conscience but has also gained notoriety beyond British shores.

Dartmoor was famously set up at the start of the nineteenth century to house prisoners removed from the condemned prison-ship hulks. These were often prisoners of war from England's wars with France in the Napoleonic era. Dartmoor was therefore considered a temporary solution, as the hulks had been before. Temporary solutions have two unfortunate tendencies. One is that claiming something to be temporary often means corners can be cut, leading to poor quality in the 'temporary' solution. This was the case with the original Dartmoor prison. Another trait that many temporary structures have is that the initial instigators move to new roles and retire, and their successors forget that the structure was supposed to be temporary. The temporary becomes permanent by accident and indifference. This also applies to Dartmoor. My main source about Dartmoor during the 1920s heyday of British gangs is *Prison on the Moor*, written in 1953 by Justin Atholl. It is a fabulous historical document with several fascinating photographs. Dartmoor had been going for 150 years when Atholl wrote his account of the prison. In 2021 the British government abandoned plans to close the prison by 2023 and instead stated that it would remain open for the 'foreseeable future'. This temporary prison has been operational for over two centuries and shows no sign of ever closing.

The history of Dartmoor as a prison starts in 1771. It is important to remember that Britain had no permanent prison system at that time. Hard to imagine now, because, in the common British mind, a number of dilapidated Victorian prisons cast a long shadow over current prison populations. The prisons and workhouses of Dickens in *Oliver Twist* are recognizable in prisons still open today. But these Victorian prisons were in fact an attempt to improve conditions. They were a modern invention designed to correct the wrongs of previous generations. As the British Empire expanded through the eighteenth and nineteenth centuries, and Britain still had capital punishment, criminals were either hanged or transported to the colonies. Making an encampment for convicts in the middle of Dartmoor was something of an idealistic project at a time when the public were content to let criminals languish in the hulks.

Thomas Tyrwhitt was the man for the job. He was secretary to the Prince of Wales, a man who would become King George IV. More importantly for our story, this made it much easier to get access to land on Dartmoor because it is part of the Duchy of Cornwall, where Prince William, as the new Prince of Wales, has recently inherited the land on which the prison stands. If Dartmoor is just a little remote and foreboding today, it is easy to imagine how wild and remote it would have felt in 1771.

Tyrwhitt intended his new encampment, the obsequiously named Prince Town, to be a farming community primarily. But the wild moor proved untameable, and he began to realize that building a few roads and buying some cattle could not constitute a profitable farm. The area is higher than the surrounding countryside and is frequently covered in fog. It rains more than the local average. It was a poor choice for a farm. By 1803 Tyrwhitt was desperate. A new war with France provided a new business opportunity. The channel ports quickly filled with prisoners of war and there was no space to house them. The prison was not Tyrwhitt's idea, but that of the anonymous Transport Board back in Whitehall. They approached Tyrwhitt, who quickly spotted an opportunity to revive the failing Prince Town. The land was provided free by the Duchy of Cornwall, the town was sufficiently remote from the channel ports in case prisoners escaped, but close enough that they could reach the prison within a day's march. Tyrwhitt would clearly have loved the new place to be named Princetown Prison but it was not to be. It has always been known as Dartmoor Prison. The plans were bold: the new prison was to host a minimum of 5,000 French prisoners and would cost far less than the prison hulks. The scene was set for the creation of a prison that has lasted two centuries and, after a brief wobble in 2021, seems set for many more decades of use.

Construction of the prison went off the rails immediately. Most of the cost was to pay for manual labour, which became more expensive due to the war. But materials were also in short supply. Granite was to be used for most of the building work because of a shortage of timber, and a tramline had to be laid to the quarry at Herne Hill. Much of the timber was recycled from broken-up ships to reduce the cost of what timber they needed. Perhaps the wide use of granite has helped the prison to survive as long as it has, but the costs began to rise immediately and the project came close to being cancelled before the foundations were finished.

The prison was originally due to open at Christmas 1807 but these difficulties delayed its opening until May 1809. The initial population of 2,500 French prisoners were marched north from Plymouth to occupy their new home. Despite the prison being new, its reputation quickly became one of fear and foreboding. The food was terrible, the weather was terrible, and the military population was frequently fighting and escaping in ingenious ways. It is important to remember that however bad conditions were they were a marked improvement on the prison hulks Dartmoor had been designed to replace. By the 1930s, the era of Kate Meyrick at Holloway, conditions had improved so much that one prisoner was heard to offer to accept a doubling of his sentence if he could serve his time in Dartmoor rather than Strangeways in Manchester. By the 1950s, the period during which Justin Atholl wrote his history of Dartmoor, only serial offenders were sent to Dartmoor because conditions had deteriorated significantly. The prisoners were not sent there to be reformed: this was the end of the road for those men who were considered irredeemable. Its remoteness reduces the quality of care and resources which can be provided, drawing comparisons with Alcatraz in California. As Alcatraz also found, once a reputation begins to take hold, every small misdemeanour or accident is exaggerated and publicized, thus cementing a reputation that has never faded.

Holloway

Kate Meyrick's personal account of her years as a Soho nightclub hostess also covers her lengthy prison stays in detail. Great kindness is shown sometimes between the prisoners, but the regime itself was brutal. It was designed as a miserable deterrent, but prisons' deterrent effects have always been suspect. Perhaps for the middle classes, the clerks and secretaries, the shame of a prison sentence did work, whatever the conditions in the prisons themselves. It was prison as a concept that they were afraid of, with all the attendant social stigma.

For those who operated on the edge of society, such as those who ran bars and clubs during a time when alcohol was widely seen as inherently evil, it seems that no level of prison deprivation would change their behaviour. What else could Kate Meyrick do? She was committed to her customers and nightclubs, she loved the life, she mixed with both high and low society, and she saw nothing wrong in what she was doing. The customers loved their evenings spent in Kate Meyrick's clubs.

The club owners colluded with the police to find ways to bend the licensing laws, which were so strict as to make the running of a profitable club impossible, and on one or two rare occasions, the licence holders were charged with breaches. Today, the worst penalty a licence holder can incur is a fine and loss of licence. Back in 1920 breaches were often punished by prison sentences during a period when the prison regime had changed little from Victorian times.

Kate Meyrick starts her account of Holloway by describing the terrible food. Breakfast was either a lump of bread so stale as to be like a rock, or just a ball of uncooked dough. It was served with watery, cold tea. Dinners, the main meal served in the middle of the day, were either corned beef and potatoes or rancid bacon, perhaps pea broth on other days or some bad doughy suet pudding. Whenever they got beef it was tough and virtually impossible to chew. Supper was the same awful bread as at breakfast, plus cocoa. Women were treated especially harshly. Most of them would start to lose weight on their terrible diet. The illogical remedy was to take them to hospital rather than to improve their food, which would have fixed the problem cheaply and permanently. Many prisoners were therefore in hospital who were not ill but simply becoming dangerously thin on their starvation rations. Many of the prisoners were on sentences longer than ten years, and their chances of survival were greatly reduced by the appalling conditions.

Kate Meyrick makes the point that Holloway prison was clean, even spotless, and would appear a benign environment to a visitor, perhaps even a curious politician. But the true horrors of the regime lurk below the surface, of which the diet is an important problem because of its relationship to good health. Incarceration and solitude, as we know now, is inherently unhealthy, and lack of food only makes illness more likely than it would otherwise be.

When prisoners were addressed by guards, it was by number. Kate Meyrick did not realize she was being shouted at on her first day in Holloway because she had forgotten she would be referred to only as Number 19. This misunderstanding caused her to be pushed and shoved back to her cell to make amends. She had forgotten to wear her cap and badge as well. Kate was sustained by visits from her children. Another illogical rule limited her to three visitors per month. She had eight children, which meant a rotating cast of visitors and the possibility of seeing each child only a few times per year, and through a metal grating at that. The emotional shock of these visits on Kate Meyrick, and no doubt on all prisoners, was hard.

Broadmoor

Broadmoor is another British institution with perhaps an even more notorious reputation than Dartmoor on account of it being, officially, a hospital. Only the most troubled individuals, including Ian Brady, the Moors Murderer, have been housed here, as was Peter Sutcliffe. Why is it that the moors in British culture, moors which are typically unspoilt nature, should seem so threatening?

Since the very word Broadmoor now conjures up images of evil and violence, it is even more important to start by reminding ourselves that it is first and foremost a hospital. Yes, some of the most violent individuals alive in Britain today are patients at Broadmoor, but they are also too unstable to survive in a mainstream prison. The cost of a year in Broadmoor for one patient is around £300,000 at the time of writing, which is fully five times the estimated cost of a year's stay in a high-security prison.

Perhaps Broadmoor does not feature large in our story of organized crime. These patients are too ill, or too vulnerable to carry on a successful life in the underworld. They are more likely to attack their own family due to a complicated childhood, and perhaps they were themselves victims in their early years. But as one extreme end of the prison system, Broadmoor is important. Later in the century, Ronnie Kray would come to spend time here. If prison life is hard and lonely, it stands to reason that some prisoners will develop mental health problems as a consequence of time served in prison. This adds to the conundrum of prison life: by taking people out of society to protect them and others from physical harm, how often is it that their mental health suffers, which further reduces their chances of ever returning to a more stable life? If prison does not act as a deterrent, then the chance of leaving a life of crime after a stay behind bars seems minimal. Although society would not now tolerate the physical conditions faced by Kate Meyrick, including appalling diet and sanitation, the question of mental health in prison is only just starting to be addressed. Broadmoor was an early attempt to correct the imbalance.

The first eight patients at Broadmoor were all women and they arrived from the London Bethlem Hospital, that most famous of Victorian hospitals, on 27 May 1863 by train to Wokingham and then onwards by horse-drawn coach. The Broadmoor Hospital was absolutely new and gleaming in the spring sunshine. There were never inmates at Broadmoor, only patients. Although one of these eight women lived the rest of her days at Broadmoor, dying thirty-seven years later at the age of seventy-one, there was a small chance of release. Around one in five men and just over one in three women would be released. However, release did not necessarily mean they were able to lead fully normal lives for the time, and the usual discharge process involved the patient being taken to the local asylum for less intensive monitoring. Back in 1863, the treatment chiefly consisted of regular routine and fresh air. The difficult lives the patients left behind were stressful, with poverty and other sanitation challenges unimaginable in modern twenty-first century life. Sedatives and stimulants were available but these were rudimentary and not finely tuned to any particular condition. Time, rest and low stress levels were the main treatments available.

In this short account of Broadmoor's first patients, we see that it was an extension of the Bethlem Hospital, which could not grow any larger on its inner city site. Additional wings were built at Bethlem but soon filled up. A more strategic solution was needed. Land was found at Crowthorne, a village on the Crown estate of Windsor Forest. It was remote, thereby discouraging escapes, but close enough to London to make transfer of patients straightforward. The railway was exploding in popularity and a new station was planned to serve nearby Wellington College. The site still feels remote today.

So we see that from the very moment of its opening, Broadmoor was a purpose-built modern hospital intended for the treatment of people classed as both 'criminal' and 'insane' and was the only place of its kind in Britain. These people were not merely ill but had all carried out an appalling crime, frequently on their nearest and dearest relations, and were deemed unsuitable for the growing Victorian prison system. Perhaps this is why Broadmoor, beloved of serial killer documentaries, hardly features in the mind of the professional gangster. Although they were all criminals, they were not insane.

Chapter 9

In Context: Early Twentieth Century

The criminal underworld of early twentieth century Britain cannot be understood without an awareness of the social and political times. Before radio and television, the newspapers were the main source of information. The stories chosen by the papers reflected society rather than an objective or scientific assessment of the crimes being committed. Working class heroes wrote even fewer books than they do today. Within these limitations, we can still get a good assessment of some important trends. Most importantly, the popular understanding of the Edwardian seems to be misplaced. Roy Hattersley's *The Edwardians* is a very good and recent account of the times for those interested in digging into the details. We find that the Roaring Twenties, which sits alongside the concept of the idling Edwardian gentleman, is as much of a myth as the swinging sixties. They are good labels, and useful in many ways, but they do not represent fairly the full extent of the times. For every lord swinging a croquet mallet there was a street scuttler wielding a flick knife, and probably more likely a ratio of 1000:1 with the scuttlers the higher number.

If the Victorians believed that the poor were themselves to blame for their own condition, the Edwardians slowly began to see things differently. It is interesting that an influential work, William Booth's *In Darkest England* of 1890, suggests transportation to the colonies for the poor. If the poor won't help themselves, ship them abroad was the same solution that the Victorians came up with to protect the nation from criminals. Sending trouble abroad was a cheap and easy option that seems to have been well supported by the British public. One can guess what the receiving indigenous populations would have said if they had been granted a voice. The notion of the undeserving versus deserving poor was still alive in Edwardian England, but even those harsh times deemed children to be innocent and therefore capable of salvation. Free school meals and school inspections were brought in from 1904. A House of Commons select committee report that year brought in a swathe of similar assistance including limited help for those over seventy and medical inspections of children in schools. The chocolate barons Rowntree and Cadbury made the point that good health depended on high living standards which could only be provided through regular and fair wages for employment. Everything was connected to everything else in that sense, and it soon came to be seen that crime was part of this complex matrix. These ideas were formed as the twentieth century dawned and, although very limited in scope, were the seeds of state benefits that would come to be a hallmark of the twentieth century. These gradual improvements led to the creation of labour exchanges in 1910 where unemployed workers could be matched to jobs.

After starting to raise conditions for the poor and improve the lives of schoolchildren, the Edwardians started to realize that criminal justice had to do more than punish. The various police forces were seen as ineffective and corrupt, and the press got on board to highlight every misdemeanour or slip-up by the police. 1910 was also the year of the poisoner, Doctor Crippen. He was recognized on a ship as he fled England after murdering his wife. Only that modern invention, the telegraph, allowed his passage to be intercepted so that he could face justice. Fingerprinting was another modern technique that was improved at this time, and one early success was the arrest of fifty-two pickpockets at the Epsom Derby in 1902. Although fingerprint evidence was not yet acceptable in court, twenty-nine of them were found guilty of other offences by relying on alternative evidence. Just a few months later, however, a Denmark Hill burglar became the first person to be convicted on the strength of fingerprint evidence alone.

Roy Hattersley's study of the political and social side of Edwardian life highlights the case of Charles Bulbeck, a twelve-year-old boy, who found himself sentenced to the cane and *six years* in a reformatory, a sort of youth prison, for the heinous crime of stealing some fish. This case is noted because the sentence was so severe, and it even caught the attention of Home Secretary Winston Churchill. He was not quick enough to stop the birching but he did get the boy released into the care of his parents. The case highlighted an obvious trend for those who cared to investigate matters: it seemed to be only the poorer boys who were ensnared by the police and law courts. Such a petty crime would have been shrugged off by the higher classes, no doubt with a few coins to the victim to offset the offence and no more would be said. Precise causes cannot be generalized in all cases, but the fact was that most of the British prison population came from the working classes, and it was not because they were naturally less trustworthy. Perhaps the working classes, struggling through difficult times, had more temptation to steal, but the government of the time understood that the real explanation was that the law treated the working classes in a different way. The less money you had, the more likely you were to receive a severe prison sentence for any given crime. Winston Churchill focused his mind on reducing the prison population. He realized that the imprisonment of youths aged sixteen to twenty-one was generally unfair and unjustified. Churchill took the view that reducing the prison population was good for the whole of society, not least because of the costs of keeping people out of action. Prisons could not hope to rehabilitate prisoners in the terrible conditions of the time. Prisoners could not earn money or be useful to society while incarcerated, and they were more likely to be there due to inadequate means of legal defence than for any sense of justice. Hattersley notes that Churchill was successful: in the ten years after Churchill became Home Secretary, those in prison for non-payment of fines fell from 100,000 to a mere 20,000. Other segments of the prison population also fell. At this time, Churchill was seen as a champion of the working man.

While these prison reforms were happening, and the labour exchanges created, the modern old-age pension began. It was the 1908 budget that finally brought it in, after that year's TUC conference carried a unanimous motion on the same topic. The plan was to introduce the pension on 1 January 1909 and, although the plans were watered down, the old-age pension did come into effect, set at five shillings a week for the over-seventies. The TUC had hoped for the same amount for everyone over the age of sixty, but it was a start. The Edwardians continued a tradition which is more famously applied to the social and welfare reforms after the Second World War. Here we see some key welfare pillars being put in place *prior* to the First World War. There were also improvements to schools at a time when very few working-class children would move up into secondary schools; their parents preferred them to start work as soon as their elementary or primary education was complete. The Edwardians, for all their faults, brought in many modern social policies.

Poverty

A common foundation for gang life is poverty. And in the 1920s and 1930s poverty meant something even more serious than it does today because life in general was harder, even for people who considered themselves middle class or working class. There were fewer electric appliances of any kind, even the basics such as fridges and washing machines. They were slow to arrive in most houses and one can imagine that they were more for show and status signalling than practical use in the early days. Everyone kept their houses spotlessly clean, an important status symbol then as now. But, at this time, cleanliness involved hour upon dull hour of repetitive manual work and it was invariably carried out by the mothers of large households. All day, every day, the routine was packing the children off to school, shopping for food, cooking food, and cleaning the house, clothes, and the children themselves when they returned home from school. The level of cleanliness needed was more than the work of a full-time job. Poverty quite often meant the parents going hungry to feed their many children. In the rarer cases, the children went without clothes and shoes to allow enough money for food. And in the extreme cases, the children would die of starvation or, at least, diseases associated with malnutrition and insanitary conditions.

Within these constraints, it is easy to imagine how the children were left to fend for themselves in a way not seen today. Even in my own 1980s childhood, the children in our street would head out from home straight after school and not be seen again until the evening meal. In the summer, we would head back out again straight after that and not be expected to account for our whereabouts again until it was time for bed. Nobody asked where we had been, as long as we came home at the agreed time. Nobody worried unless we were over half an hour late. Our own 1980s gangs were non-violent and were more like friendship groups. We would play various games like conkers and football or go to a friend's house to watch television. It seemed to us that as long as wherever we went we kept moving, we would not get into trouble or come to harm. And in all those long childhood years, we never did.

Fifty years before that it is clear that the children, and boys particularly, were left to organize their own entertainment in the evenings and at weekends. It is easy to see how, with high spirits and the wrong role models, harmless friendship groups could turn to criminal activity, even if only out of boredom and the best intentions. Easy to see how, if your parents lost interest in your whereabouts, perhaps because they were fighting for their jobs and against their various creditors, the boys could lose their compass. Poverty for the parent could lead to negligence of the children, who always test the limits of discipline even in the best-behaved examples, and the longer they are without guidance from parents the more likely they are to seek alternative role models in older siblings. If such siblings are routinely smoking, drinking and whiling away time with knives and other illicit items the rest is easy to imagine.

Put another way, it is difficult to imagine someone turning to criminal gang activity in the *absence* of poverty. The causes might be many, they might be complex, and they might be interlinked, but without the catalyst of poverty they are unlikely to lead to trouble with the police. The exceptions to this are rare.

In Flora Thompson's well-loved account of an Oxfordshire village at the turn of the twentieth century, *Lark Rise*, she states that, 'Early in the [eighteen-]nineties some measure of relief came, for then the weekly wage was raised to fifteen shillings; but rising prices and new requirements soon absorbed this rise and it took a world war to obtain for them [the villagers] anything like a living wage'. No doubt pay would have increased without the impetus of a war, but it would likely have taken years longer to reach the same level.

Disenchantment

If the roaring twenties was more of an American tone, touched less severely by war, the mood in England was summed up in a single word: disenchantment. This was the title of a famous 1922 book by Charles Montague. It vividly captures both the sense of thrill that accompanied the first volunteers to fight the Great War in France, and the rapid downfall in their spirits when reality set in. At first the whole thing seemed like a summer camp for adults, although many were under twenty. They were just the sort of men who might have been attracted to gangs: hard workers, underpaid, looking for adventure. The sense of duty erased any sign of doubt. They signed up with friends and colleagues, whole families and production lines at a time. They signed up with a smile, but those who returned were never the same again. This sample of *Disenchantment* gives a flavour: 'A child who has rashly taken its parent on trust, and yet more rashly taken the parent's all-round perfection as some sort of sample and proof of a creditable government of the world, must have a good deal of mental rearrangement to do the first time the parent comes home full of liquor and sells the furniture to get some more.'

This is a sad, haunting book. The real haunt comes from our knowledge that an even more terrifying war was due just seventeen years after this book was published, which means that the babies being pushed around as Montague wrote these words were the very ones who fought the second great war. *Will we ever learn* might have been its subtitle because Charles Montague himself finishes the book by reflecting that everything in life happens in cycles and, even as he hopes war will not return he anticipates that it will after memories of the terror fade.

Growing Up in the City

In an important 1954 work by John Barron Mays, *Growing Up in the City*, we find delinquency and gang behaviour described as a 'social tradition' because it is just one aspect of a way of life. Those who exhibit delinquent behaviour tend to be, and seem invariably to be, those who grow up in the oldest parts of the largest cities, whose families have been poor for decades or even generations, who struggle to find regular employment and find themselves living in squalid housing. Sometimes factors such as cultural conflict and religious division are added to the list of symptoms or causes. Children in these areas find themselves less well educated, possibly even encouraged to leave school prematurely to earn a living, and with limited access to recreational facilities. Put against such a context, it is hard to imagine a child succeeding in this environment to break into the middle classes. There are so many social forces pulling them back, largely from within their own families, but also from their peers and other intrinsic health and poverty factors, that they are far more likely simply to continue the tradition of their ancestors.

It is true that, even in such disadvantageous beginnings, not everyone becomes a delinquent but if the background is combined with certain personality traits, that outcome feels inevitable for the minority who join up with gangs. The studies considered by John Barron Mays show that if recreational facilities are provided, the groups of youths do tend to self-organize into clubs and take advantage of the provided facilities. The spontaneity factor is important: if the leaders select themselves from within the neighbourhood, rather than being imposed by a well-intentioned town council or committee, the results are more positive. If the bad influence can come from within the home, then fathers who volunteer to lead youth groups have much more influence on the minds of their children and their children's friends than outsiders ever could. Perhaps surprisingly, organized religion did not have such a marked impact on the likelihood of boys to become delinquents.

Small adjustments can have a big impact. Some of the studies looked at in Mays' book found that boys would not steal from the elderly or from one-person shops. They would not steal from people they knew. Similar behaviour was found in the military: each new intake would steal from each other before personal friendships were formed, when the pilfering would cease. In the largely middle-class grammar schools, pupils were given responsibilities to look after desks and lockers, and ownership of books. The more wealthy boys were therefore taught the importance of ownership and pride as a matter of routine. These privileges were absent from the primary and secondary modern schools in urban areas. These studies, which modern sociologists and historians could no doubt find fault with in terms of methodology, confirmed that the poor were not to be blamed. Such a complex network of cause and effect stretching back generations, when coupled with a certain personality, was virtually certain to result in delinquency. In most boys it was a phase that passed before adulthood but in others it persisted. And conversely, it is easy to imagine that a strong-willed middle-class boy, if subjected to the same pressures and temptations, would also tend towards delinquency. A later section of the study shows that in fact all groups of boys misbehaved from time to time, but middle classes had ways to shield their youth from the criminal justice system which were not available in poor areas.

Mays suggests that a court appearance for a missing bicycle lamp is not only a disproportionate way to treat such a minor misdemeanour, but punishment by magistrates from outside the immediate area might actually cause a worse response in the unlucky child than more supportive chastisement from parents and teachers. Of course, more caring and thoughtful processes cost money in the short-term, are hard to explain to the wider law-abiding and voting public, and then, as now, are more likely to be pilloried in the media than a hardline approach.

This series of academic studies carried out in the years before 1954 show that the causes of delinquency were well-understood at the time and would have been just as easily understood decades earlier. A combination of difficulties in the economy and society at that time meant the public had more urgent matters to attend to, and the unfortunate harsh realities faced by the urban poor were not high up their list. That a few Edwardians, and a few from each subsequent generation, were able to see solutions and improve the lives of many young delinquents is reassuring and impressive. But they could not shift that striking image of the wanton criminal, the lad so hard of heart and fixed in his behaviour that no punishment could change his behaviour.

Mays emphasizes that delinquency, and gang behaviours, are only one aspect of underprivileged neighbourhoods. They are the oldest, and poorest parts of the city, and their low-paid jobs and bad homes have been around for decades. One persuasive reason why young people in those areas join gangs is the element of social tradition. A boy joins the gang of his older brother, who copies their father, who learned from his older brothers and their fathers and the friends of their fathers. Mays goes slightly further and claims that 'it is only a very few youngsters who are able to grow up in these areas without at some time or other committing illegal acts'. Most might only commit one or two ad hoc crimes, but it is easy to imagine how a significant minority of such young men would routinely commit crimes or join gangs or enjoy regular violence. The gang is part of the fabric of these areas, and these areas are large enough that they contribute something to the fabric of the wider city, leading to stories in newspapers that terrify the population of the other, better off, areas, who are typically at little to no risk from the gangs they fear so devoutly.

The studies showed that it is comparatively easy to modify the tendency to commit crimes. Modest clubs and games, organized if possible by parents from the local area, can have a big impact on the crime levels and delinquency levels far beyond the local area. In some cases, helping young men to understand the impact of their activities on their victims was shown to reduce crime. As Mays puts it, if a boy can 'visualize the consequences of his actions' then he is less likely to be violent towards others. Mays even shows that there are times of the week, and quite short ones, when the risk of crime and violence peaks. At the time being studied, the worst moment of the week occurred on Saturday morning. With no school or church to attend, children wandered unsupervised, stealing from shops and market stalls. Mays suggests this as the best time to hold a club or event for the boys. This Saturday morning tradition is still followed by football clubs across the country, and it is no coincidence that the professional game really took hold after the Great War. The game was becoming more popular, and more boys were playing it in clubs at the weekend than ever before. A fascinating appendix looks at the organization of Sunday football in an area of Liverpool, at Jericho Farm. Even more striking is that this area is still used for sports and is home to South Liverpool FC today. This book teaches us many things, and one of them is that decisions of a century ago can still be paying off a hundred years later. Back then, there were three main groups involved in football on a Sunday morning, with boys starting at the age of fifteen, and including men of all ages. There were no marked pitches and the goals were made of piles of coats, just as we used to play football, and no doubt every other generation in-between. Refereeing was carried out by the players themselves, with captains enforcing the rules. Teams were generally drawn up from residents of a particular street or tiny area of the city. Teams brought their own balls and played in regular clothes. There are so many small details here but the theme for me is that it required virtually no money to arrange or hold these football matches. The ball was the only specialist equipment. The key to the success of football at Jericho Farm, on the bank of the river Mersey by Aigburth Vale, was that it was self-organized by local residents for themselves and their children. It can be imagined that the two large fields, which are described as hopelessly overcrowded and chaotic, could hold hundreds of young men on any given Sunday. It is less likely that the same teenagers and their friends would become delinquent with such a compelling and competitive club thriving on their doorstep.

And this was a time when the Scouting movement was widely popular too. The *Belfast Telegraph* of 4 December 1935 describes the local picture. In 1935 there were sixty-six Scout Groups in the county borough of Belfast within which there were 1,138 boys in the Wolf Cubs (now more commonly known simply as 'the cubs') 1,397 in the Boy Scouts, 515 Rover Scouts (now the 'Venture Scouts') and around 300 adult leaders and assistants. The scouts organized a summer camp for boys who would not otherwise have been able to experience a family holiday. Cups presented at the organization's annual meeting show that a wider range of sporting activities had been held: football of course but also swimming, signalling, and an ambulance cup.

Mays is under no illusions as he draws his compelling study to a conclusion: 'No single nostrum is likely to be found which will solve the problem [of delinquency] once and for all. It is probable that some form of delinquency is endemic to our modern civilization with its commercial lures, its mechanization, its mass conditioning and detachment from any morality higher than opportunism and economic advantage.' Mays was writing this in 1954, but he understood that the drivers of change in the second half of the twentieth century had already been set in train.

Chapter 10

Female Gangsters, Part One

There were often significant differences in how the genders approached organized crime. The exceptions to these trends are the stories that catch our eye, like the female face slashers of the Forty Thieves syndicate led by Alice Diamond. The social upheavals of the 1920s would probably have occurred later and more gradually without the war, but the war changed expectations of women, not only their expectations of themselves, but also how the male-dominated society viewed their role. If women could farm fields for long hours, if they could staff production lines, even lines making deadly weapons, maybe there were other jobs they could do. Perhaps the factory owners found that the women worked a little harder, with fewer mistakes and even fewer complaints than the men they replaced? When the men returned, they were mainly able to take up their old jobs, and the women went back to the sort of roles they would have tolerated before the war. But the door had been opened. Young unmarried women, yet to have children, might choose to stay on. And even if they didn't fancy the noisy, dangerous factory, there were other opportunities now beyond the drudge of domestic service. And for the very few, like Alice Diamond's friends, there were still more exciting ways to make money.

Perhaps the best way to understand the differences between female and male organized crime is to start from this point, the point of social expectation, and work forwards. The male gangs first began organically in overcrowded streets with few social outlets. Perhaps things got started with a brawl after a long session at the pub, which led to a grudge, which led to a rematch. Maybe someone went too far and someone's older brother joined in. The link between male gangs and boxing, or bare-knuckle street fighting, is strong. As the gangs became more formally defined, with one or two leaders and a semi-regular membership, ideas began to build. Given that gangs have always been part of society, it is impossible to be sure exactly how things started. But there are observable cycles to gang violence and the peaks tend to occur in times of social upheaval, when there is insufficient work, or the wages are too low, in areas affected by poverty. There are trends and it seems to be the poverty aspect that tips the gang over from being a social gathering or club, towards being a way to subsidise low wages, and eventually to becoming a well-run professional criminal network.

The simple explanation is usually the right one. Perhaps the business models of the male gangs, and it is not too grand to call them business models, evolved naturally out of the things they knew and enjoyed. Gambling was a surefire way to make money, if only the risk element could be reduced or removed. Running short cons, such as the spinning jenny, three card trick or hunt the ball in the cups, could all be rigged to ensure that the house won every bet. But how long before the punters began to realize and stopped playing? These were the shortest of short cons, but the direction of travel was set inexorably towards the racecourse. Gambling away from the course was illegal, but in high demand, so any bookmaker brave enough to take and lay bets in a pub or street corner was breaking the law. The local residents did not see it as such, they saw it as a useful service, and it was one of those many laws that society generally saw as unfair at the time and tilted against the working class. The rules were made by people far away in Whitehall who had no idea what working class life was like. At certain times, the police would crack down on these illegal betting pitches as it was an easy way to show that they were clearing up the streets without making much effort. In turn, the bookmakers got more savvy. They chose to take bets from locations with several exits, and in footpaths between houses or at the end of culs-de-sac so that they could not be spotted from a distance. A further improvement was to send children round the pubs to collect bets and return winnings. If they were caught, they would be let off by the police on account of their youth and the bookmaker would be able to continue work the next day. Eventually, the small ambitions of the local bookmaker made it too difficult to turn a profit, or the profits that could be made at the racecourse itself were far greater. And this is really when the balance tips from being a small time enterprise on the verge of illegality, to genuine organized crime. Rather than take the time to learn the form and build up a bookmaking business, the gang leaders found it easier simply to beat up the legitimate racecourse bookmakers and steal the large amounts of cash they had to carry around to conduct their business. Even easier was to merely threaten the bookmaker so that he would hand over a small portion of his profits. It avoided the personal risk in beating him up, which would attract the police, or possibly a group of bystanders keen to uphold justice, and the bookmaker could hold onto most of his money. As more gangs moved in, they would compete for the bookmakers. They would act tougher than the other gang to get the bookmaker to pay them the protection money instead, or they would slightly wound a bookmaker who was paying a rival gang as a warning. Before long, it was a real threat not only to the profits of the bookmakers, who found more and more of their money disappearing in these illegal taxes, but the law-abiding race goers noticed an element of chaos and danger at the largest race meetings. The problem became so great at the largest race meetings such as the Epsom Derby that the horse-racing organizers and track owners began to recruit their own security guards. In a farcical decision, they turned to the very hoodlums who had been threatening their business, and the guards used appalling violence on the gang members, raising the stakes even further.

We can see how physical violence was a hallmark of the male-dominated gangs. Any working man of the time would have been able to handle himself in a fist fight. Trouble could break out without warning and sometimes running away was not possible. Right from the beginning, the female career criminal was more intelligent and strategic. They could in theory train themselves to win a fight with another woman, but a rival gang could simply hire some more experienced fighting men to protect them. The women would have to be more calculating.

Just as the men had settled on gambling as a way to wealth, so the newly trained female domestic servant, exposed to a wealthy townhouse or country mansion for the first time, would be dazzled by the clothes and jewels on display. Some quiet pilfering was unlikely to be noticed and, if it was, the family would not want to involve the police. Scandal was to be avoided at all costs. As long as she avoided stealing the heirlooms, a determined maid could supplement her poor wages without reprisal. Alternatively, a girl going into the mills instead of domestic service would train as a seamstress. This taught her the value of silk fabric, which would become important when selecting rolls of material or ready-made dresses later in her criminal career. It also gave her the skills to adapt her own clothes for the concealment of contraband. An extra pocket here, a slit there, an extra belt, and you had a flowing dress that could carry large amounts of other dresses away from a department store undetected. Once the war came, those girls who did not manage to find work in the war effort found that their sewing skills could be adapted. The female criminal gang, perhaps better described as a syndicate, brought together a wide range of different skills and personalities. A few of the women enjoyed violence and could be used for protection when things got sticky, but most would use their experience of working for the upper classes, their confidence in society, to beguile the unsuspecting department store assistants. If men were used, they would likely be the chauffeurs of the getaway cars because society would not notice a man at the wheel of a car. Another role for men in the female gang was to fence the stolen goods as reputable dealers or shop owners who asked no questions.

This very simple, if not simplistic, overview of the different approaches to crime by men and women shows that it was not completely down to free will. The expectations of society led them into certain roles or jobs, which gave them certain skills, and meant that women could walk into a department store unnoticed, skilfully stripping the shelves of their finest dresses. A man would stand out in the same situation. The men, trained and experienced in fighting, were far more likely to threaten violence to get the money they needed to make ends meet.

Not long into any journey into female crime, you are likely to encounter Carol Smart's landmark book of 1976, *Women, Crime and Criminology: A Feminist Critique*. From the beginning, Carol Smart re-confirms that shoplifting is a crime associated with women, and the crime most likely to be carried out by women. We find that women predominantly steal items associated with a stereotypical female role. Household items, make-up, clothes. The former might be stolen out of necessity, but gangs like the Forty Elephants chose the best clothes because they brought the biggest profit. A further point made by Carol Smart is that the high fashion any eligible young woman would seek was expensive and far outweighed the pittance available to most working class women. How were they to afford such items? They either had to persuade a man to buy a dress or steal it. There were no other options.

The Forty Elephants

The first sources I found about female gangsters were in obscure academic journals. They referred to the portrayal of feminism in *The Sopranos* TV series. There was only one book-length work in the whole library: there were a couple of useful chapters in an ambitious tome entitled *Selling Sex in the City: A Global History of Prostitution, 1600s–2000s*. It felt like the whole endeavour was the result of a bet around the use of a famous sitcom. I hadn't expected it to be easy to find good material on the role of women within gangs, but this was a frustrating start.

It turns out I was not alone. Caitlin Davies relates a similar story in her introduction to her brilliant *Queens of the Underworld*. I found this book during my hunt for news on the incredible-sounding 'Forty Elephants' gang. Although male gangsters and criminals outnumbered the women, it is also the case that their stories have been told more often, magnifying the imbalance. This line of thought led me to question again what the definition of a gangster really is. Brian McDonald calls the Forty Elephants a crime syndicate. That sounds more precise than calling them a gang and implies a level of professional detachment. To the Forties, shoplifting was a meticulously organized business activity.

The most common crime for a woman, judging from the newspapers, journals and books, is that she murders one of the men in her life, typically her husband or boyfriend. This is the most common crime for men too, incidentally. In second place comes burglary, a crime of choice rather than self-defence, and it is much less likely that a woman will enter into the sort of joint enterprise that is an important component of the male gang. That is why the Forty Elephants stand out. Their story reaches back into the nineteenth century when they were known as the Forty Thieves. The personnel changed over the years, and perhaps there were never forty of them at any one time, but this female crime syndicate were expert shop lifters on an industrial scale and had the hallmarks of a gang. They were professionally run and did not shy away from violence when it was required.

Mary Carr

Mary Carr is the name which most commonly begins any account of the early days of the Forty Thieves. Mary Carr was born in 1862 and she was only ten when her mother died. It is easy to imagine how hard life must have become when, four years later, she had her first brush with the law for shoplifting. In the workhouse she joined her brother and two sisters. Mary Carr's father, John Carr, was an enthusiastic criminal. Caitlin Davies discovered that he was once found with £1,000 worth of bonds stolen from a ship. Mary was charismatic and famous for being good looking. It was not long before other girls started to follow her. After she left the workhouse in Kent, she returned to London as a flower seller on the Strand. This was known as a cover for prostitution but Mary's growing band of followers had slightly different ideas. One of the girls would lure a wealthy gentleman by innocently asking for directions. He would walk with the girl to show the way, after which a number of her accomplices would appear and accuse him loudly of assault. Rather than face a scandal, the gentleman would usually hand over his valuables to avoid a scene. These were crimes of cunning, a form of blackmail or short con trick, and they were highly successful at a time when a gentleman would go to lengths to avoid association with the street girls. It is possible that this group of women were initially tied to the better-known Elephant and Castle gang, but Mary Carr's leadership and charisma allowed her to take charge of her own independent gang.

Mary Carr was so famous during her life that she is reputed to be the model for a number of famous paintings and also the inspiration behind the play, *The Worst Woman in London*, by Walter Melville. She died in 1924 after an eye-opening varied career spanning thirty years. Mary's tragic childhood and criminal father led some to label her as a 'born criminal' but from our vantage point we know there is no such thing. Her intelligence and beauty allowed her to excel in a man's world at a number of different careers, as a model and muse, as well as a pickpocket and short con artist. Her leadership skills ensured her legacy would continue. The Forty Thieves needed a new leader to take them through the 1920s.

Alice Diamond

Alice Diamond stepped forward to take this role. She was a charismatic leader like Mary Carr. Fashion conscious and outgoing, Alice's interwar Forty Thieves knew how to enjoy themselves. They specialized in immaculately planned and executed shoplifting raids in the most fashionable stores of London's West End. This was an era when children grew up fast, especially those lower down the social ranks. Alice worked in domestic service from the age of fourteen. This work provided numerous temptations to poor girls who were suddenly exposed to vast wealth. She was only sixteen when she had her first experience of the police for shoplifting. By the age of nineteen, in 1915, she found herself sentenced to a year of hard labour in Holloway Prison, the conditions of which have been described in detail by fellow prisoner Kate Meyrick.

At nineteen, Alice Diamond was already crowned the latest queen of the Forty Thieves. She was an expert in physical disguise and used pseudonyms to evade capture. Many of the Forty Thieves had experience in the textiles industry. There were plenty of jobs for working-class women, although they were poorly paid. This not only gave them a sense of fashion and an ability to understand which rolls of fabric might be the most valuable to steal, but some of them had tailoring skills which allowed them to make voluminous skirts in which to hide stolen goods. They adapted all kinds of dresses, coats and other items by adding hooks and belts, allowing them to carry off surprisingly large amounts of contraband undetected. Caitlin Davies found that there might have been as many as 10,000 professional female shoplifters by the end of the 1920s in London. Solo operators would not count as gangsters, but this is a surprising number given how few of their stories are remembered today.

London law enforcement gradually got to know and understand the Forty Thieves well enough that the women became notorious. As with all successful enterprises, they had to adapt and expand and they began to target other towns and cities as far north as Manchester. More than anything else the girls wanted to enjoy their earnings and they would dance and drink in the best clubs, including Kate Meyrick's 43. It was at this time, at the height of their achievements, that this incarnation of the gang became known as the Forty Elephants. Alice had a relationship with Albert McDonald, a member of the Elephant and Castle gang. The Forties gang even paid subscriptions, like a voluntary tax, to ensure they had money set aside for legal advice and other contingencies. They were a true professional outfit, and highly successful. They could be just as violent as their male counterparts too, with Maggie Hughes, Alice's sidekick in leading the gang, accused of slashing the face of Ethel Martin with a razor.

According to Brian McDonald, whose ancestor Albert had a relationship with Alice Diamond, Alice's childhood was chaotic. She was born in Lambeth Workhouse on 20 June 1896. Alice had around ten different childhood addresses as her family moved from place to place in London. Her father was often in prison and she barely went to school at all, as schooling was not compulsory or free at the time. Whether or not this counts as being born into a life of crime, Alice was certainly born into poverty. Her story travels through the ages due to an unusual combination of factors. Why do we know so much about Alice and not about the thousands of other poor children born at that time? She was unusually tall, perhaps five feet ten inches, although newspapers usually rounded this up to six feet at a time when the average height for an adult woman was nearer five feet, and even a typical man would stand only five feet six inches tall.

Alice had repeated brushes with the law, which was one of the few ways a working-class woman could get her name into the historical record. She was stunningly beautiful, which meant she got noticed in any situation. And she was businesslike in her criminal activity.

The Great War perhaps nudged Alice towards a life of crime. As the large houses cut back on domestic servants, many of the girls would have found well-paid work in munitions factories as the men went into battle. Brian McDonald has found evidence that Alice did indeed seek work in a munitions factory, but this ended when she was convicted of using false references to get the job. Tantalisingly, the job might instead have been a crude attempt to obtain explosives. Alice's brother had been arrested for trying to obtain raw materials such as fertiliser for the purposes of making explosives for blowing safes. In a fabulous quote from the time, brother Tommy was described as 'the brother of the cleverest woman shoplifter' in London. Alice was already the most famous member of her family.

One of the most striking aspects of the Forties gang was its brazenness. The gang was so successful that they needed two fleets of cars. After the girls had stuffed several cars full of stolen goods, they were driven back to base to be checked and fenced by recognized specialist dealers and retailers around the capital. A second fleet of cars would return to the West End to be loaded with yet more contraband.

The confidence of the gang was striking because punishments were severe by modern standards. By this time the trouble was so bad that the grand department stores of Selfridges and Harrods were being criticized for virtually encouraging theft by placing piles of valuable items on open display for customers to touch and try out. It is notable that the shoplifters targeted department stores, with goods on open display, rather than jewellery shops, who closely guarded their more valuable items and kept them locked away as much as possible. The department stores did not want to employ visible security guards as they thought their presence might deter their sensitive and wealthy customers. Eventually, theft became so rife that it began to erode profits and action was taken. The stores recruited female operatives of established private detective agencies such as Madigan & Kemp to go undercover, thereby providing a novel if niche career for women. Annie Betts became so effective and notorious in this role that she became known as the 'Lady Sherlock Holmes' by the *Daily Herald*. Most culprits were opportunists who stole out of desperation, of course. Alice Diamond was shoplifting royalty, rare but all the more memorable for it.

One important element that held the Forties together was teamwork. The Forties excelled because they had each other's backs, most of the time, and tried to uphold their revered 'Hoister's Code' which held them together when their leaders were in prison.

Once the female detectives hit their stride and the police started to recognize gang members, as with all successful businesses, a change in tactics was needed. The Forties hit the provinces. They travelled to Manchester and beyond but found that shops in smaller towns were easier to turn over. Such outlets were thrilled to have posh-voiced visitors from London in fancy cars with drivers and enthusiastically opened themselves up for short cons and flagrant shoplifting.

The arrival of the Great War in 1914 caused a hiatus in the activities of both the casual shoplifters and the career thieves like the Forties. For those who stole out of desperation, new jobs were available in munitions factories and other war-related jobs. They were well paid, much better paid than domestic service, although nowhere near the earnings of professional gangs like the Forties. As with all trends and patterns, the drop in shoplifting during the war could only be explained by a number of different causes. Surely not everyone in the land was able to work in a noisy, dangerous factory, no matter how high the wage. Shoplifting must have continued. But now the wares were not as plentiful or as thrilling. With bare essentials at risk of running out, and factories concentrating on weapons where they could, the volume of luxury items dropped off. And once the crisis passed, the newspapers stopped worrying about it.

If the war years were lean for the Forties and other professionals, there was a rebound once the war ended. The lead up to Christmas of 1919 was a big year for shoplifting. Society found that it had pent up demand for luxuries. After years of hardship, people were better off. They had been paid well during the war and when the goods returned to the shelves, they flew off them again just as quickly. Some new faces arrived on the West End shoplifting scene and Alice Diamond returned to the fray as the undisputed queen of the Forty Thieves gang.

By the 1930s the male gangs were becoming highly specialized and audacious. Perhaps they would not have been so successful as shoplifters. The Forties women were partly successful because nobody expected women to steal so blatantly. Perhaps also the men were attracted to the technical complexity of true burglary. Rather than walking into an open shop, they were more likely to organize a raid on a closed jewellery shop. The smash-and-grab raid was the most simple and relied on brute force and a quick getaway.

The 1930s saw no let up in the activities of the Forties, even though the police had been lying in wait when they arrived in Birmingham. Police officers stationed in provincial towns had successfully captured some of them during the Christmas sales. Policing was becoming more sophisticated and focused on pre-empting plans rather than just being reactive to a crime happened upon by chance. As a result, the shoplifters had to improve their tactics.

It is hard to define precisely who was a member of the Forties because it was a loose network. Was Dorothy Mays one of the syndicate when she appeared at Cardiff Assizes in June 1930? She stood accused of crimes committed in far-flung locations that included Cambridge, Hull, Halifax, Reading and Manchester as well as Cardiff. Dorothy Mays was the sister of one Maggie Hughes, whom Brian McDonald states was a firm member of Alice Diamond's Forties. Maggie's husband Alfie was known as a bookmaker, which at this time was so often code for various kinds of gang-related crime. If the women were shoplifters, their men tended to be described as bookmakers.

The *Halifax Daily Courier* reports that Maggie Hughes turned up in court again in November 1934, this time at York Assizes for shoplifting a coat and three dresses from shops in nearby Hull. When Margaret Lilian Hughes was sentenced to four years' penal servitude, she and her accomplice became hysterical. This sentence took in a range of other crimes in Lincoln, Peterborough and Grimsby. Nevertheless, these were harsh penalties.

The Second World War brought with it another lull in shoplifting activities. Not only were all the familiar alternative wartime jobs available once again, but bombs were falling on London to devastating effect. Laws were brought in to deter looters and these even harsher penalties could be applied to shoplifters too. The balance of risk and reward was no longer attractive to the hard-headed business brains leading the Forties. Some shoplifters tried their luck in the provinces once again until rationing brought clothes coupons and the quantity of fine dresses and luxury items dropped off again as the country focused attention on the essentials. Some of the best targets for West End shoplifters such as John Lewis and Bourne & Hollingsworth were destroyed by bombs.

Alice Diamond's hold over the Forties ended with the war. A new leader emerged and, although Alice retained allegiance to her gang,

Brian McDonald suggests she was more of a backstage arranger and figurehead rather than the active day-to-day leader of shoplifting sorties. This time the press and wider society blamed dim lighting for the return of the shoplifters. Stringent war rules limited the amount of energy that could be used for lighting, which was seen as a luxury, even in business premises. Poor lighting was just one more small entry to add to a very long list of explanations for large-scale shoplifting. Although there are reports of Alice working as late as 1947, she began to suffer from ill health and died at the age of fifty-five on 1 April 1952. She was replaced as the leader of the Forties by Shirley Pitts, who led the gang through the 1960s. Shirley also died comparatively young at the age of fifty-seven on 16 March 1992. But it was Alice's skill in building up, recruiting and training such a large band of skilled pickpockets which made Shirley's tenure not only possible but perhaps more stable.

One inescapable point is that the Forties were famous in their own time, perhaps the female equivalent of the Krays. Variety hall singer Nosmo King sang about them and they even made the news in America. There was a radio play based on the gang and also a West End play.

Chapter 11

Female Gangsters, Part Two

Once you get beyond the lurid newspaper coverage of female gangsters, and the brilliant career of Alice Diamond and the Forties, it is possible to discern a re-evaluation of the female career criminal. As recently as 2016 Charlotte Wildman published an academic paper about a conceptual figure she called Miss Moriarty, after Sherlock Holmes's nemesis. She draws attention to a clear trend in modern media and society at large: the idea of the woman as the victim, and the crime or criminal being depicted as inherently masculine. Charlotte Wildman explicitly considers the inter-war years, which makes this a good source for our purposes here.

We discover that crime committed by females hits the public conscience at the same time women are moving into paid jobs that were traditionally filled by men. The men, of course, have gone to France or even further away to fight the Great War. There are so many unusual events triggered by war that the precise chain of cause and effect is not possible to figure out definitively. And it would not have been exactly the same for each individual. Crime has always looked attractive to a certain type of mind placed in specific constrained circumstances. Did more women turn to crime because their bread-winner was away, and they were thrown into poverty? Or was it simply because it was a lawless time, comparatively, and crime was less of a social sin? Probably both are true, and lots of other combinations besides. It is likely that the war contributed to this particular social upheaval, the notion of the woman not as the moll of a male criminal, but as an independent criminal mind in her own right. War started a chain of events that would certainly have happened later without the war. As society discovered electricity, it seems that some of the first appliances to take advantage were in the home. Refrigerators, washing machines, vacuum cleaners, the electric iron. The canny salesmen realized that the woman trapped in the home could be a powerful ally in persuading her husband to buy the latest tech. And once the daily grind was simplified women had more time on their hands. They were bored. What better and more modern thing to do than find part-time work, or piece work that could be carried out in the home around other tasks? From that position, it was only a matter of time before women applied for jobs in offices and factories, with or without the war.

It is important to keep in mind that punishment for female crime rose only 20 per cent during the inter-war years and from a very low base. Whatever the angst in the newspapers and public discussion, the issue of the female criminal was dwarfed by the vast number of crimes committed by men. Thus the need to strike a balance between ensuring that the female side of the history of British gangsters is remembered, and possibly in some sense celebrated, yet at the same time understanding that one reason it is not as strong in the memory now is because it was never that much of a genuine problem at the time. The Alice Diamonds and Kate Meyricks were exceptions, but fascinating and compelling ones.

It is at this time that the notion of the beautiful female criminal really comes to the fore both in movies and novels, but also in the newspapers. The appearance of female criminals was exaggerated if there was an element of beauty. Contrasting that to the classic description of a male criminal, who is more likely to be depicted as an out-and-out thug of frightening appearance. Thus the trope of *femme fatale* was born: the wolf in sheep's clothing, the Trojan horse. The beautiful woman who will poison your drink while distracting you with a smile. What more terrifying prospect is there for a man? It remains a powerful character trait and story line in books and films such as *Red Sparrow*. Yet the chance of this actually happening to someone was virtually zero.

An unexpected point noted by Charlotte Wildman that the notion of a beautiful and expensively dressed female criminal, perhaps wearing jewels too, was so common in the press that this sort of character description in fiction became an indicator that the woman so described was either one of the baddies or, at the very least, somehow morally deviant, such was the strength of the stereotype that emerged between the wars. Wildman further notes that Agatha Christie, still the undisputed queen of crime, who rose to prominence between the wars, balanced her killers roughly equally between the genders. However, Christie also tended to make her female criminals beautiful and fashionable. Make up and cosmetics were becoming more affordable and common at the time, so these also became hallmarks of the female master criminal. It seems that everyone was making their female criminals attractive, and the myth is still with us.

Just as war was blurring the gender boundaries that had become firmly established in British society for decades, it brought hard times for the aristocracy too. High death duties and other burdens led many wealthy families to reluctantly contact the fairly recently established National Trust to see if they would help out. They were not necessarily willing to sell the whole property, but some would allow weekend visitors during the summer as a compromise. The Trust acquired its first house in 1896 but really expanded and entered the national consciousness between the wars. It is no surprise that we find there were many female criminals who tried to hide their intentions by not only dressing well but even using the names of wealthy aristocrats as part of their con routines. But male criminals engaged in this sort of basic subterfuge too, including pretending to belong to one of the professions, such as law or medicine. The only clear difference between the sexes is that the women are depicted as playing up their beauty and using it as part of their disguise.

As international travel became cheaper and easier, this element also crept into the stereotype of the *adventuress*, a woman who was essentially an exotic con artist who was able to blend into any social situation. This stretches belief. The probability of an expensively dressed woman drowning in jewels, able to fake the mannerisms and speech of the aristocracy while also funding foreign trips to northern France, perhaps le Touquet, was more like a fantastic international spy than someone who could ever exist in real life. If she had the education and money to pull all that off, why would she resort to the risks associated with crime at all? What a fabulous character for a movie, but not someone you were ever likely to meet.

Josephine O'Dare

I came across the brilliant character of Josephine O'Dare while researching a cheque-fraud case. One of the fraudsters, Benjamin Harper, would steal cheques from post-boxes to persuade a bank to issue a replacement chequebook to him, and was involved in something the newspaper called 'the O'Dare group of forgers'. Intrigued by the idea that there could be a whole series of forgeries conducted by a single group that made national news, I began to dig. There are parallels between the lives of Josephine O'Dare and Kate Meyrick. They trod different sides of the same line, some might say. Whereas Kate Meyrick travelled to London from Ireland and, falling on hard times, worked her way into the nightclub business, Josephine O'Dare travelled from Ireland to London where she worked her way into high society, perhaps attending Meyrick's clubs as a customer. When she fell on hard times, she turned to forgery and cons. She built a team of men around her, a forgery gang requiring a number of different specialist skills, but O'Dare soon found herself in Holloway Prison at around the same time as Kate Meyrick.

Josephine O'Dare was as cunning as the Forty Thieves, although there is no connection that I could find. Whereas the Forties were expert shoplifters, O'Dare built her own forgery gang. The crime that led to her spending three years in prison during the years leading up to 1930 was the forging of the will of an associate, a solicitor called Edwin Docker. O'Dare had been a close friend of Docker to the extent that, according to her own serialized life story, he had agreed to give her £20,000 to offset some business debts she had from deals which had collapsed. Unfortunately, Docker died before he could make good on his promise. Josephine O'Dare had seen this gift as her last chance to avoid bankruptcy proceedings, a belief that later proved true, so she arranged for Edwin Docker's will to be forged, naming her as a beneficiary to the tune of £15,000. This case was so notorious that it was reported far beyond London and became a national story. Stories appeared in *The Scotsman* and in local newspapers across Britain. The will forgery seems to have come to light only after O'Dare and her associates had been caught forging cheques and using the will document itself as security on other small loans. O'Dare had mixed with the very top tier of London society, including members of parliament and the son of a duchess, and had persuaded a solicitor to pretend that he had witnessed the will of Docker. She also described one of her male friends as 'the famous American antiseptic king' who was probably Jordan Wheat Lambert, who licensed the formula for Listerine mouthwash from Joseph Lawrence, a chemist based in St Louis, Missouri.

In her column on 3 August 1930, headlined 'Mayfair's Marriage Market', Josephine O'Dare is scathing about the 'market' for young women propagated by their own mothers. The high society world O'Dare entered in London was one in which mothers would cynically find the richest and most titled young men to whom they would attempt to hitch their daughters. It went beyond the political manoeuvring seen in Victorian novels. Matchmakers would be employed for cash to help grease wheels and make introductions, sometimes between the least compatible of individuals. One older woman, whom O'Dare does not name, was supposed to be a wealthy catch, suitable for even the most eligible young bachelor, but O'Dare gradually discovered that the woman so highly sought after was not wealthy at all and lived off an allowance made by anonymous older admirers.

Josephine O'Dare claimed credit for working as an intermediary on a number of substantial business deals. She understood the business principles and would ask detailed questions about a business proposition before agreeing to make introductions between the ideas men and the money men, who were often titled gentry. Her persuasive skills seem to have been her sharpest asset and, coupled with a confidence to mix in the higher circles, she does give credibility to the idea that she legitimately raised tens of thousands of pounds for her own use. Her business acumen did not extend to spending the money shrewdly, and it was a debt for £15,000 that ultimately caused her downfall and imprisonment. So keenly did she feel the untimely death of Edwin Docker, her most recent benefactor, before he was able to transfer the money he had promised her, that her determination burned hot and she cast aside the moral compass she claimed to have in her popular series in *The People*. These articles ran through July and August of 1930, once a week on a Sunday, and the newspaper was widely rumoured to have paid £800 to Josephine for the privilege.

Kathleen Cooper

One week after Josephine O'Dare's popular series concluded, the appetite for similar articles was so great that *The People* published an article by Kathleen Cooper, who had served a long prison sentence alongside Josephine O'Dare in Holloway. Kathleen Cooper describes how she moved to England from Belfast at the age of sixteen and easily forged a cheque for £2,000 with which she travelled to Dublin and lived the high life until her money ran out. She travelled to Glasgow and then later, with a friend, to London. When they collected their paltry luggage from Euston, they discovered that security around the luggage area was non-existent. By giving a false name and a good story they later gained access to six large suitcases which they unpacked in their hotel. Most of the goods were related to a shop move and were worthless, but they obtained enough high value items to raise some money. Cooper had trained in leatherwork and found it easy to obtain raw materials on credit from a number of suppliers. The business was difficult, and she could not make back the money to pay for the materials. Her friend was in service and through her connections they gained access to various grand houses which they proceeded to rob. Cooper's point in this article is that, although she accepts the blame for her role in these various crimes, the temptation faced by a penniless woman in England on her own was great, but her ability to obtain money was facilitated by so many people, nearly always men, who would gift or lend money or provide credit based on word of mouth and the flimsiest cover story. Such an article might have scandalized many readers because it devalues honesty and blames people, especially the great and good, for being overly kind. Although as Kathleen Cooper states, it is not really kindness at all: 'They come for a variety of reasons – through sheer thoughtlessness, or carelessness, and, sometimes, through the seeking of a new thrill.'

Kathleen Cooper's childlike claim to be a victim is transparent and would have no doubt angered the readers of *The People* but, at the same time, a whole generation of criminals found cheque fraud to be an easy way to raise funds at very little risk. It seems to have been so easy that there must have been countless cases where the perpetrators were not caught, or at least caught too late to recover the money. Society had been founded on honesty and integrity, but those with money had been flouting it in front of hired servants who could not have dreamt up such luxuries before entering service. As with the street gangs of young men, there would always be a sizeable minority of young women willing to chance their arm at theft. Kathleen Cooper's argument is that, although it was easy to blame and imprison her as a criminal, it would be better if those who flaunted their wealth were less gullible. Admittedly, when I first read about the crude nature of the cheque fraud which led me to Kathleen's exciting life story, it was the lack of security checks which stood out. It was a crime so basic, viewed by modern standards, when more of society ran on trust and the word-as-bond principle, the only surprise was why more people didn't attempt it. These were difficult times, between two appalling wars, with vast gaps between the wealth of the classes. There was no wonder a few adventurers tested the limits of their luck. Viewed another way, forgery takes a particular degree of skill that those of a non-artistic temperament might partly envy. Imagine being able to create bank notes, cheques and letters that are indistinguishable, in the hustle and bustle of a bank or shop, from the real thing, and using the money to correct a perceived wrong. Probably no reader of *The People* would accept Kathleen's protestations of innocence fully, but probably quite a few had sympathy in their hearts as they read about her difficult early life.

The pattern of poverty leading to temptation and then, for a minority, leading to a cynical and organized criminal life is roundly criticized in the newspapers of the time, then as now. But the picture posts, the salacious stories and attention-grabbing headlines were bought in their millions by people to whom buying a daily or weekly paper, or even both, was not considered expensive. Very few of the readers would have to struggle to save up for a copy of some throwaway newsprint, yet the Kathleen Coopers of the world knew what it was to go hungry, when the cost of a newspaper would have seemed like extravagant wastage.

Chapter 12

Weapons: Knives and Guns

We have seen that knives and other sharp instruments were favoured by British gangsters, with guns used only occasionally. There were many reasons for this. One was simply availability, and guns were more prominent in the years after the Great War as they filtered back from the front lines through various back channels. But there was another factor. With the death penalty still frequently used for murder, use of a firearm could get the killer the ultimate punishment. By limiting themselves to knives, and by careful use of those knives, the gangsters knew they would not hang. Tampering with witnesses by threats of violence made a conviction less likely too.

The experienced gangsters would even take precautions in how they held a knife, such that the main aim was to hurt and disfigure the victim. The blade was held so that a fatal injury, perhaps to a major artery around the neck, was prevented.

Priya Satia's excellent book *Empire of Guns: The Violent Making of the Industrial Revolution* makes one point very clearly: it was war that drove the industrial revolution. Without the machines and mills there could be no empire, but the more subtle point here is that it was war that provided the momentum for those machines. Between 1688 and 1815, a period of 127 years, Britain was at war for a total of eighty-seven years: nearly 70 per cent of the time. And when Britain was not at war, it was either recovering from one or preparing for another.

Thus guns and heavy weaponry were vital, but even more peaceful industries such as textiles and agriculture were significantly employed in making supplies for Britain's armed forces. Virtually no industry was exempt. This was the period when the Royal Navy not only ruled the waves but also had significant political power. Britain's influence was growing, yet it was war that provided the impetus. Virtually anyone in private industry could find their wares being deployed in one war effort or another. A pacifist might find it difficult enough avoiding conscription, but such a conscientious objector would have found it even more difficult to avoid working for a business that was at least peripherally involved in supplying one war or another.

At this time, society was fairly open to the use of guns in the protection of property. A shopkeeper defending his business against marauding gangsters would have been justified to defend himself with weapons. Guns were in that sense a status symbol of the time. The mere knowledge that one shopkeeper possessed heavy weapons would make his shop less prone to attack. The government had always regulated guns as far back as the fourteenth century. Regulation implied permission: guns have never been outrightly illegal in Britain.

One way in which Britain significantly reduced gun use was to make the penalty for murder the death penalty, virtually guaranteed, with no long and uncertain legal appeals process. The fear of execution does seem to have caused even hardened gang members to prefer the knife. If guns were carried, it was as a warning and a status symbol rather than for practical use. Once created and sent abroad for use in war, the life of the gun was long, theoretically unlimited, and it would inexorably find its way back home and into private hands. The myths and reputations of highwaymen and smugglers also date back to this time and live long in the memory.

Not surprisingly, the major cities where guns were made became centres of the gun trade. Priya Satia recounts the story of one T. Richards, a Birmingham gunmaker, who sold all kinds of guns from his high street shop, although his signage was focused on the use of guns in sport. This confirms that, as the eighteenth century dawned, guns were getting just a little too easy to obtain. Society and government's views on guns varied with the times. During times of rebellion, gun laws became stricter. But during more peaceful times, the availability of arms and private militias was seen as a way to underwrite the security of the state. At times when arms were available, they were only available legitimately to the middle and upper classes. Not only did the British government vacillate over the use and availability of firearms, but the British public seemed reluctant to use them even when they were widely available. We have seen how knives were the weapon of choice for gangsters but, even during riots, when guns were available, the masses would often choose farm implements, pokers, bricks and stones, swords, cutlasses, catapults – virtually anything *except* a gun would make an impromptu defensive weapon. Proof of this are the occasions when gunstocks were used as thrown projectiles: the very guns themselves were dismantled for hurling, rather than being used to fire bullets.

Even when riots broke out between gun workers at a Birmingham gun factory, no bullets were fired. On another occasion, a crowd grew to protest the royal reprieve from hanging of John Porteus, captain of Edinburgh's City Guard, who had been arrested for ordering his men to fire on a crowd. The demonstrators acquired the guns and other weapons of the City Guard so that they could not be used against them. The demonstrators took it upon themselves to hang Porteus and left the guns behind when they left his cell.

The British were singularly reluctant to use guns at all. They were hardly ever used in murder or suicide. Priya Satia recounts some anecdotes from Gloucester which saw one accidental shooting in 1739 which arose between quarrelling boys during which one was shot by mistake. She found two accounts of deliberate shootings in the 1740s and a suicide by shooting in the 1750s.

In London in the eighteenth century there were only two to five cases of deliberate shootings each decade. Pistols were far more likely to be used as a heavy object to beat someone than as a shooter of bullets. Perhaps the reluctance of the British people to use bullets during these decades stemmed from the image of the gun as an ungentlemanly weapon. It was simply immoral to shoot someone who was not equivalently armed, and guns were only used to intimidate and worry an enemy. In that respect, guns were used far more freely than they could be today.

The exception to this reluctance to fire a gun was the duel, which was a highly orchestrated social encounter in which all kinds of rules had to be followed, not least the stipulation that both men required pistols. Even in these dangerous performances, people were rarely killed due to the pressure of the situation, the unreliability of the guns that would often not fire at all, and the dodgy aiming of the amateur gentlemen.

It was the early years of the nineteenth century, when the working classes had fought wars in large numbers, that our attitude to guns changed. Guns were being fired by new groups of people and for different reasons. No longer sporting gentlemen, or landowners frightening poachers and burglars, we begin to see rioters using guns in a way that would never have happened a century earlier. People began to try carefully and methodically aiming the guns for the first time. James Hadfield, a silversmith, fired at King George III more as a protest than a genuine assassination attempt, and another shooter was successful in killing the British Prime Minister Spencer Perceval in 1812.

There is an interesting footnote to the changing image and use of guns as the nineteenth century approached the twentieth, the period under our consideration in terms of the gangs of British cities. Birmingham companies such as Birmingham Small Arms (better known today as BSA) perfected the creation of small arms on an industrial scale for the Great War. But as the war ended they were left with stockpiles which nobody would buy. Just as they had done before the First World War occupied their production lines, they diversified into making cars and bicycles, a decision which would eventually make BSA one of the best-loved motorbike manufacturers in Britain. By the 1930s the ability of Britain to make its own weapons was at risk of dying out, and it was only the threat of a new war in the middle 1930s that reversed the trend for diversification.

The rifle is a well-known yet misunderstood weapon. No use for close combat, and most closely associated these days with sport, it was an important military weapon during the early years of the twentieth century and a brief look at the rifle helps us to further understand the times. Terry Wieland is a life-long hunter, and he has distilled his knowledge of rifles into the entertaining *Great Hunting Rifles*. Terry unashamedly describes rifles as though they are people with their own unique personality and soul.

The feature of the rifle that gives the gun its name is the *rifling*. To understand the need for this, it is first necessary to understand that a rifle is primarily a long-range weapon. Snipers today, with the latest equipment and lots of practice, are able to shoot accurately for at least a thousand metres. To achieve accuracy over that distance is hard, but it would be impossible without rifling. The inside of the gun barrel, the long tube from which the bullet shoots, is marked with spiral grooves. As the bullet fires along the inside of the barrel, these grooves impart spin. The tighter the grooves, the more the bullet will tend to spin. The more it spins the more stable it will be in flight, and the more accurate the weapon. Thus the rifling, the grooves, within the barrel gives the gun its unique properties.

A good rifle, as for any good gun, is a result of a number of difficult trade-offs. A bullet that fires fast will cause a lot of damage. But will its aim be straight? A spinning, stable bullet might be accurate, but will it travel as far? How accurate is the sight? How easy is it to pull the trigger? It should not be too easy, but not too stiff either. Terry Wieland suggests that making the perfect gun is as much an art as a science. Some of these factors include the length of the barrel, the grooved rifling, the size and shape of the *stock* or handle, the dimensions of the bullet or cartridge, whether the rifle has a telescopic sight to improve accuracy, but which can also get in the way in a hurry, or the *action* which is the way the projectile is made to move.

It turns out that the highest quality weapons had to be handcrafted and could not be mass produced. But the weapons, not only rifles, needed for the Boer and Great wars had to be turned out in huge numbers by mass production lines in great factories. So the guns of the time were not amazing. They could be unreliable and they were certainly inaccurate. It was liable to blow up and injure the shooter without warning. The quality of bullets was similarly unpredictable. On the other hand, the simple knife could not go wrong. Even a blunt knife had the capacity to injure. A damaged gun might look good until you tried to use it in a jam, and then it would not work. Add to this the social stigma around the gun not being a fair weapon, or not being a gentleman's weapon, and then add the legal framework which handed out the death sentence should anyone die during a fight, and it is much easier to see why guns were never favoured in Britain. They were simply too unpredictable. Good to carry as a deterrent, but never to be fired.

George Alexander Myford's unprovoked shooting of Maud Webb, a nursemaid, attracted headlines in September 1913 as it drew attention to the reportedly widespread use of 'Derringer' type pistols by gangs. 'In order ... that the public might know the very serious consequences that might arise from the reckless use of pistols, the Magistrate committed the accused for trial', stated the *Western Mail*. Myford was only twenty-one and it is clear that the process of holding a trial was partly a way of highlighting the growing problem. The circumstances are shocking and show that it was never the case that gangs only ever fought under gentlemanly rules against the declared members of other gangs. The implication is that the young woman was used for random target practice: 'The girl's evidence was that when passing a coffee stall in Harrow Road the defendant, who was with six or seven other young men, discharged the pistol and shot her in the back. She thought it was done "just for a joke".' Myford denied the injury to Maud Webb was deliberate but the edited highlights in the *Western Mail* give the impression that the shooting was a deliberate act. However, a more nuanced and detailed account in the *Sevenoaks Chronicle and Kentish Advertiser* feels a little closer to the truth. Maud Webb was with a friend when they walked past the coffee stall and one of the young men knew her, shouting out 'good night'. After she replied, a shot rang out and she felt it hit her. She described the gun as being 'six inches long'. The 'just a joke' comment was in reply to the magistrate asking if she thought she was shot deliberately: 'No, I don't think so,' said Maud. 'I think it was done just for a joke.' The paper goes on to suggest that there was a good-natured exchange between the men and women before Maud was shot by accident: 'One of the prisoner's companions explained that there was "a little joke" going on among the young fellows, and after the two women had gone by laughing, the prisoner fired the pistol to make them jump ... Sergeant Hall stated that when arrested the prisoner said he intended to shoot on the ground, and only did it for fun, not knowing that the cartridges were dangerous.'

Afterword

In writing this book, I followed a path wherever the sources took me and I tried to avoid ground covered so well by experts in the field including Carl Chinn, Dick Kirby and Brian McDonald. Quite early on, I resolved to cover cities outside London, the less famous gangs, and the female gangsters. Prison featured as a heavy shadow in their lives but is rarely covered in other books on gangs. And I try to show that gang behaviour was most often a complicated combination of circumstance with personality and that the vast majority of gang members were not irredeemably violent but in some cases got trapped in a lifestyle they tried in vain to escape. This book should not be seen as a comprehensive coverage of gang activity in Britain and Ireland in the fifty years to 1950, but the result of fascinating hours in the library and in the newspaper archives.

In some aspects of gang life, I managed to find some empathy. I could understand how a society deeply scarred by war, with most of its men trained in the use of knives and guns, would be more violent than British society today. I knew that death was more a part of life than it is now. Mothers would lose babies and, indeed, children of all ages could be carried away by an accident with a hot bath or a coal fire, or any number of infectious diseases. The workplace, whether it be the mine, the farmer's field, or the factory or mill, was dangerous. People worked six days a week and they were long, noisy, hot and difficult days. Industrial accidents of all kinds were common, and many could prevent someone from working or even kill them. For men and women, life expectancy was in the mid-fifties.

These were dangerous times. I could understand how a gang fight might end in accidental death, or even deliberate death. There was perceived to be something honourable in a fair fight, whatever the outcome. But the death penalty was irreconcilable for me. At least we had moved beyond the days of hanging as public entertainment, as the British death penalty in 1868 moved behind closed doors. But it was not until a century later, in 1964, that Britain would finally turn its back on the punishment. There is nothing clean or quick, or humane about the death penalty, however it is carried out, and I found the cold calculation of rope lengths and drop heights abhorrent.

I have been softer on the gangs than some other writers because I could see that for a minority of people with certain character traits, with different life experiences, faced with the desperation of never-ending poverty, crime would come to seem a viable respite, if not a true solution.

I hope that this book has gone some way in showing that they were mainly troubled people scratching a living during turbulent times, having fought in a war so terrible that everyone in the country was affected by it for the rest of their lives. The war accelerated changes that corrected injustices in British society, changing the relationship between men and women, and starting the erosion of the British class system that held so many people back. We have a lot to thank these people for, in all kinds of ways, and we should try to understand how and why a very small number of them turned to professional crime and violence. In understanding the notorious gangsters as well as the hundreds of other less famous gangs, we can understand the wider society at the time, and even the underpinning of our society today.

Acknowledgements

This is my first non-fiction book and it has given me new admiration for the many other writers whose work has guided me through a topic that was new to me. I strongly recommend all of the books in the bibliography.

All the books written before 2000, and all the articles, were found in the London Library, which is a gem of a place for all those who love books and history. All the newspaper articles were discovered in the British Newspaper Archive, which is a brilliant project providing an essential service.

Thanks to Jonathan Wright and Charlotte Mitchell at Pen and Sword for their patient advice throughout this process, and for the helpful suggestions of my editor, Richard Doherty. A special thank you as well to Brian McDonald who kindly allowed me to incorporate some of his amazing photographs.

And thanks most of all to my wife, Becky, and daughter, Isis, who have provided support and encouragement when the finish line seemed so far away.

Bibliography

Books

Atholl, Justin, *Prison on the Moor: the Story of Dartmoor Prison* (J. Long, London, 1953)

Booth, William, *In Darkest England, and the Way Out* (C. Knight, London, 1970)

Chinn, Carl, *Peaky Blinders: The Real Story* (John Blake, London, 2019)

——, *Peaky Blinders: The Aftermath* (John Blake, London, 2021)

Davies, Andrew, *City of Gangs: Glasgow and the Rise of the British Gangster* (Hodder and Stoughton, 2013)

——, *The Gangs of Manchester* (Milo Books, 2009)

Davies, Caitlin, *Queens of the Underworld* (The History Press, Cheltenham, 2021)

Hattersley, Roy, *The Edwardians*, (Little, Brown, London, 2004)

Johnson, W. Branch (William Branch), *The English Prison Hulks* (C. Johnson, London, 1957)

Kearns, Kevin Corrigan, *Dublin Tenement Life: an Oral History* (Gill & Macmillan, Dublin, 2006)

Kingston, Charles, *A Gallery of Rogues* (Paul and Co. Ltd, London, 1924)

Kirby, Dick, The Racetrack Gangs (Pen and Sword, Yorkshire, 2020)

Kobler, John, *Capone: The Life and World of Al Capone* (Joseph, 1972)

Mays, John Barron, *Growing up in the City: a Study of Juvenile Delinquency in an Urban Neighbourhood* (University Press of Liverpool, 1954)

McArthur, Alexander, and H. Kingsley Long, *No Mean City: A Story of the Glasgow Slums* (Longmans, Green, 1935)

McDonald, Brian, *Alice Diamond and the Forty Elephants: The Female Gang That Terrorised* London (Milo Books, 2015)

——, *Elephant Boys* (Mainstream Publishing, Edinburgh, 2000)

——, *Gangs of London: 100 Years of Mob Warfare* (Milo Books, 2010)

Meyrick, Kate, *Secrets of the 43: Reminiscences by Mrs Meyrick* (J. Long, 1933)

Montague, C.E. (Charles Edward), *Disenchantment* (Chatto and Windus, London, 1922)

Rodriguez, Garcia, Magaly, et al. *Selling Sex in the City: A Global History of Prostitution, 1600s-2000s* (Brill, 2017)

Satia, Priya, *Empire of Guns: the Violent Making of the Industrial Revolution* (Duckworth Overlook, 2018)

Smart, Carol, *Women, Crime and Criminology* (Routledge, London, 1976)
Thompson, Flora, *Lark Rise* (Oxford University Press, 1940)
Trail, Armitage, *Scarface* (A.L. Burt Company, New York City, 1930)
Treherne, John, *The Strange History of Bonnie and Clyde* (Cape, 1984)
Wieland, Terry, *Great Hunting Rifles: Victorian to the Present* (Skyhorse, 2019)

Articles
Wildman, Charlotte, (2016) 'Miss Moriarty, the Adventuress and the Crime Queen: The Rise of the Modern Female Criminal in Britain, 1918–1939', *Contemporary British History*, 30:1, 73–98, DOI: 10.1080/13619462.2015.1055254
'Gangster Feminism: The Feminist Cultural Work of HBO's "The Sopranos"' Author(s): Merri Lisa Johnson Source: *Feminist Studies*, Summer, 2007, Vol. 33, No.2 (Summer, 2007), pp.269–96 Published by: Feminist Studies, Inc.
'Commodifying the Self Within: Ghosts, Libels, and the Crook Life Story in Interwar Britain', Author(s): Matt Houlbrook Source: *The Journal of Modern History*, Vol. 85, No.2 (June 2013), pp.321–63 Published by: The University of Chicago Press

Online
Inflation Data https://www.officialdata.org/uk/inflation/1922?amount=500000
Bank of Liverpool Limited 1831–1919 from the Barclays Group archives https://archiveshub.jisc.ac.uk/search/archives/f93dde5b-48d6-380c-b98b-764b8ddbc4ea

British Gangs

British Gangs

From 1900 to 1950

Paul Dettmann

PEN & SWORD
TRUE CRIME

First published in Great Britain in 2024 by
Pen & Sword True Crime
An imprint of Pen & Sword Books Limited
Yorkshire – Philadelphia

ISBN 978 1 39907 387 5

A CIP catalogue record for this book is
available from the British Library

Typeset by Mac Style
Printed in the UK by CPI Group (UK) Ltd, Croydon, CR0 4YY.

FSC MIX
Paper | Supporting responsible forestry
FSC® C013604
www.fsc.org

Pen & Sword Books Limited incorporates the imprints of After
the Battle, Atlas, Archaeology, Aviation, Discovery, Family History,
Fiction, History, Maritime, Military, Military Classics, Politics,
Select, Transport, True Crime, Air World, Frontline Publishing, Leo
Cooper, Remember When, Seaforth Publishing, The Praetorian Press,
Wharncliffe Local History, Wharncliffe Transport, Wharncliffe True
Crime and White Owl.

For a complete list of Pen & Sword titles please contact

PEN & SWORD BOOKS LIMITED
47 Church Street, Barnsley, South Yorkshire, S70 2AS, England
E-mail: enquiries@pen-and-sword.co.uk
Website: www.pen-and-sword.co.uk
or
PEN AND SWORD BOOKS
1950 Lawrence Rd, Havertown, PA 19083, USA
E-mail: uspen-and-sword@casematepublishers.com
Website: www.penandswordbooks.com